F E R

IAN FERGUSON

WITH

KEN GALLACHER

FIRST PRESS
PUBLISHING

Fergie

Published by First Press Publishing,
Daily Record and Sunday Mail Magazine Division,
40 Anderston Quay, Glasgow G3 8DA.
© First Press Publishing

ISBN 1-901603-08-3

Printed and bound in Scotland

W0010089

CONTENTS

This is for my family who have supported me throughout my career. I cannot thank them enough.

IAN FERGUSON, SEPTEMBER 1999

FOREWORD BY DAVID MURRAY, CHAIRMAN OF RANGERS

IAN FERGUSON is probably the last man for some time who will be given a Testimonial at Rangers, and also in the whole of Scottish football.

He is the last of an era, the last of a breed, if you like, as the game moves forward and away from players who spend most of their careers with a single club. He is a Rangers man through and through but he is also a highly respected professional as regards opposing clubs. When he has been out of our team there has always been interest from around the country from other clubs who would like to have him in their squads.

We are just delighted that he has been content to stay with us. This is now the day for hired professionals, for players who will come in and do a job for any club for the length of their contract and then they will move on. Ian is not like that. He was someone who always wanted to be at Rangers.

He has always played for the jersey and that has been admirable and he has won as many medals as anyone after being here during the most successful period the club has ever enjoyed. I know that has given him satisfaction but he deserves all the success because of the contribution he has made over the years he has been with Rangers. I was delighted to give him a Testimonial because I know the support have a great, deep feeling for him.

1

CHAPTER ONE

A Dozen Years For Me – But Rangers Will Go On Forever!

It is now more than 125 years since Rangers Football Club was founded yet, in all that time, the period between 1988 and 1997 gave the team the greatest period of sustained success it has ever experienced.

I count myself very fortunate to have been a part of that run and fortunate, too, to be there as one of the stepping stones between that era and the new one which the Dutch coach, Dick Advocaat, has kicked off so spectacularly by winning the domestic treble in his first season in command. The near dozen years or so I have spent with the club have been turbulent ones and when I study the team I played in when I made my debut against Dundee United on February 27, 1988, just 12 days after I had been bought from St Mirren, I realise that I am the sole survivor from that game which we drew 1-1. The team was Chris Woods, Jimmy Nicholl, Jan Bartram (who remembers him now?); Graham Roberts, Ray Wilkins and Richard Gough; Derek Ferguson, myself, Scott Nisbet, Ian Durrant and Mark Walters. In fact, the only man still around Ibrox who was there when I joined as a player is the reserve team coach, John Brown. The changes have come about because Rangers have always chased success and Graeme Souness set the pattern which Walter Smith followed of moving players on whenever it appeared that their position could be strengthened by going into the transfer market.

Following that came the Bosman ruling which opened the game up for players, giving us the kind of freedom which people had talked about for years but none of us had ever believed would happen. For my generation of players it seemed that the game would be in danger of collapse without the recognised transfer system. My own experience underlined that when St Mirren paid £65,000 to Clyde for me – a sum which kept the smaller club in cash for some time. Then the Love Street side sold me to Rangers for a fee of £850,000 plus some extra bonus payments after I had been capped by Scotland and that money kept St Mirren solvent for a period. It was the way the world of football went round.

Small club discovers young player and allows him experience to develop his skills. Big club sees him, buys him and allows the less wealthy team to survive on the transfer cash. Suddenly all of that changed and while there are still transfer fees, the way in which the system works does allow players the opportunity to walk away from their clubs at the end of their contracts. The long-term hold that clubs always had over their players has gone and it has led to a wage explosion for footballers which has made many of them wealthy but it's my opinion that the size of the salaries now being earned is forcing more and more clubs into debt as they constantly try to find success. Don't get me wrong, I am not criticising any of today's star players for the money they earn. I don't envy them the high salaries they now collect and I don't grudge them the money either. The post-Bosman system is in place and the judgment when it was made in Belgium was done in the manner it was so that players could benefit after the many years when too many of them – Jean Marc Bosman included – were exploited because the contract system was so biased in favour of the clubs and football's ruling bodies. You could not argue with that but I doubt if the judges realised that the demands of players and their agents would reach the levels of today.

The Bosman ruling has not affected me because once I joined Rangers I never really wanted to leave and I hope now that the day doesn't come when the club will decide that I have outstayed my welcome. I realise that it is possible to carve out a new career after being allowed to leave Rangers, as Ian Durrant and Ally McCoist and Andy Goram have shown recently. But I have had indications in the past that other clubs wanted me and I made it plain that I did not want to move on because I have never really wanted to play anywhere else. Now I have never been one of the top earners at Ibrox. Mind you, I thought my ship had come in on the day I was offered my first contract by Graeme Souness. I had been earning something like £220 a week at Paisley with bonuses on top. A couple of years before that with Clyde I was getting £45 a week! Graeme gave me £700 a week for a four-year deal and that also included bonus payments for weekly wins and any trophies which might be won. Fine, St Mirren had just won the Scottish Cup but that was scarcely the norm.

You did not have to be any kind of genius to recognise that the bonuses at Rangers were going to arrive with a great deal more regularity than they ever did at Paisley. And trophies were the same. At first I could not grasp what had happened to my wages. With bonuses added they were liable to have risen more than 20-fold in the two and a half years since I left Clyde. Ever since then I have, I think, been fairly easy for the Chairman to deal with over contracts. In essence, I have a figure in my mind and then I see the Chairman and talk things through and when we reach agreement I am happy to accept what has been outlined. If someone then goes in and gets a lot more money than I do, then good luck to them. I don't feel the slightest bit of jealousy because I have made my own deal and I don't let anything else affect my feelings.

The point I am trying to make is that there are players around the game now who will make more in one season than I have earned in all my years at Ibrox. Now that's fine because I recognise that times have changed enormously and the wages with them but the long-range concern is whether the clubs will be able to sustain the salary levels which are now on offer. It would not affect the major clubs, Arsenal and Manchester United down south and Rangers and Celtic in Scotland, because the level of support is so great and the revenue from season ticket sales and merchandising has grown beyond all belief over the past few years. But the lesser clubs who have ambitions to challenge the top brand names are those who might be in some kind of financial danger. The major worry is that television walks away from the game because that would cause serious problems in England where the Premiership deal has financed the spending in the transfer market and the salary hikes which have both been so remarkable in the last few seasons. I know the argument will always be that footballers have only a short career and I realise that as well as anyone because I am nearing the end of my own footballing life. But without healthy clubs how will football continue? If top-level clubs end up in bankruptcy – and it almost happened to Celtic a few years ago remember – the whole game would plunge into crisis. I just happen to think that agents should lower their sights a little and realise that, yes, there are clubs who cannot afford to pay a star player £20,000 a week.

However, there are many more clubs who will be tempted by the thought of signing a big, big name yet will not be able to afford that type of money. The warnings are there for all of us to see. My former manager, Walter Smith, joined Everton last season after he left Rangers and within a few months discovered that the Goodison club was in financial crisis – one which had to be resolved by selling players. Now, just as no one would have believed Celtic's plight five years back, similarly no one would have thought that Everton, one of the great names in English football, a club with a tremendous history, would also be flirting with disaster. Yet that was the case and no doubt other clubs are in the same position as they continue to chase success.

In Scotland, of course, it is different because only the Old Firm can compete at the top end of the transfer market and only the Old Firm can afford to pay top dollar when they bring in big name international players. The other clubs – and none of them will like me writing this – only exist by hanging on to the coat tails of the Big Two from Glasgow. Rangers and Celtic keep the rest of the Premier League clubs alive. They attract sponsorship. They attract television contracts. They attract the biggest crowds and while grounds are smaller than they once were the appearance of Rangers and Celtic at any provincial stadium means a sell-out. And remember, that means FOUR guaranteed sell-out fixtures each season which is a considerable boost to their finances. Anyone who does not agree with my assessment should ask themselves if the television companies would be paying out big money for the Scottish fixtures if the Old Firm were not there. The answer is simple. They would not be interested in investing the same cash as they are doing at the moment. Just look at the schedules and count the number of times that the two Glasgow teams are on the box in live matches and that will underline my argument. Our supporters had very, very few Saturday games to watch at Ibrox last year with so many being switched to the Sunday night slot for showing on Sky. That was what the television company wanted and that was what the viewing public wanted and that will not change because the lure of the Old Firm will always be there.

The one problem the two clubs often share is the difficulty of attracting some top-quality players to the Scottish League.

Many of the players from the Continent see Scotland as a little bit of a backwater when compared to the hyped-up Premiership down south. I don't think the English League is as good as they claim it to be. For the most part, however, there are bigger grounds around the whole country and bigger crowds at most of the games, though Rangers and Celtic are closest to Manchester United for the highest average attendances in Britain – something which should not be forgotten. Still, I think that if the Old Firm is going to continue to grow and to flourish then they would have a much better chance of doing so if they were playing in the English League week after week. European players who are coming into our domestic game need bigger and better challenges and you can sense that some of them don't enjoy going to some of the smaller grounds we have up here. The general level of play is higher but I reckon that the Old Firm would soon be challenging at or around the top of the Premiership. I spoke to Walter Smith last season and he agreed with that. His view was that there were one or two outstanding teams, Manchester United and Arsenal and Chelsea for example, and then the others were all of a certain level. He thought that the Old Firm would be able to compete well in that environment. We would become better teams and we would be able to gauge our progress better game by game than we can do at present. It would be a much better yardstick for the players and for the coaches who have to use the European games just now to assess the standing of the teams accurately in a more global sense rather than just in our own goldfish bowl. If we played there, then it would also make it easier to persuade players to sign because they would know the level of football they were entering.

At the moment the Scottish Premier League is looked on as being of a much lower standard than the English Premiership and so players will opt for England ahead of here when a transfer is being mooted. Now I know that some of the lesser teams are capable of causing upsets to the Old Firm on certain days and under certain circumstances but that is not how the top European players view things. If it is not going to be possible for Rangers and Celtic to move into the Premiership – and I can understand that there could be problems from the English teams who would have to step down to make room for us – then Europe is the answer.

Having taken part in the initial Champions League it has been interesting to see how that experiment, which started off at the behest of the leading European club sides, has developed and how it continues to develop. More clubs seem to be taking part each year and it would appear that at some stage a European League which would guarantee the clubs a certain number of games every season – and hand the television companies a midweek football bonanza – will come about. That would solve many of the Old Firm concerns. If you were playing on the European stage week after week then Continental players would be attracted to you because they would then be able to recognise the size of the two clubs, the passion of the support and the stadiums which rival any across Europe. And, while they would be playing in the domestic League in tandem with the European competition, it would not be done in isolation and there would not be the danger which Scottish teams must always face nowadays of going out in a preliminary round to a team of some stature and then facing a bleak winter with only the Premier League as the challenge.

Change has to come but whatever happens in football I am utterly convinced that Rangers will always be a vital part of any major developments. The Chairman and Dick Advocaat have indicated that a soccer academy to bring on young players is a priority and if that is the case then it may be that even with the Bosman ruling I won't be the last player at Ibrox to notch up a dozen years of service. Barry Ferguson could do it. Barry Nicholson could do it. And there could be others out there waiting for the chance to graduate from the new soccer academy. Meanwhile, there is no doubting that the future is in safe hands. There cannot be any safer place for the club's future than with a group of players who were able to deliver the treble in the way these lads did. None of the fans need worry about what lies ahead. We might have players from half a dozen countries mingling together in the home dressing room at the Stadium but they are all united in one thing – they all want to add more and more success to the Rangers' history. They have started in the right way and it could be that the best is yet to come from the squad which has been constructed by Dick Advocaat. They are capable of providing that.

2

CHAPTER TWO

The Dream That Almost Died

Anyone who knows me at all will confirm that all I ever wanted to do, right from the time I was a youngster, was to play football for Rangers. I went to the games at Ibrox. I travelled to the away matches and my support for the team never wavered even though these were dark days for the club. Days when we had watched Celtic winning nine Championships in succession and listened to their supporters' celebrations – which was especially difficult for me living next door to Parkhead as I did back then.

You know, I can still remember all the disappointments we suffered back then, all the defeats and all the trophies Celtic won when I started off going to the games.

I grew up 50 yards or so away from Celtic Park but my Dad went to all the Rangers games and I suppose that's where I got it from. When I was really young I went with friends, Neilly McLean and Joe Hobbs, who took me on the Cross Bar bus and I went everywhere with them to see Rangers play. I think I was at every ground from Aberdeen down to Berwick with them and the other lads who went on the bus every week. I didn't get to any of the away games in Europe but I didn't miss many in Scotland.

The first game I remember going to was a reserve match at Ibrox against Falkirk and a cousin of mine, John Coleman, took me. I can't even remember the score and I certainly can't remember who played for Rangers – but I do still remember seeing this huge, huge stadium and I suppose that's when I started dreaming about playing football there.

The first game I do remember much about was an Old Firm match when Rangers were down 2-0, yet fought back to win 3-2. That was a tremendous game and the guys who played for Rangers at that time, John Greig, Tom Forsyth, Tommy McLean and Sandy Jardine, were my heroes.

Tom Forsyth and John Greig were tremendous and Greigy was an inspiration. In my opinion it was only right that he was voted the Greatest Ever Ranger when that award was presented recently. He always seemed to stand for everything that was good about Rangers.

Not only that, he showed magnificent loyalty when the club was going through really troubled times. I am certain that he could have left Ibrox and moved on to one of the top English clubs. There must have been opportunities which he could have taken but that was not his way. He remained with Rangers and for season after season he seemed to be carrying that team. There were games when he literally held them together, times when it was his defiance which allowed Rangers to get a result they desperately needed. They call him "The Legend" at Ibrox and more than anyone else he deserves that accolade. The supporters who were around back then had to suffer a lot. These were the days when Celtic were in command and when their supporters were able to do most of the singing and partying. But that did not lessen the loyalty and commitment John Greig showed for Rangers.

At the time he never seemed to make any fuss, no great song and dance about what he was doing, just getting on with the job and trying to change the course of events by his own example. No one can deny how inspirational he was and that quality alone made him a great servant to the club.

It would have been easy for him to go but he didn't and I look back on the times I watched him and I think he was one of the players I tried to model myself on. My problem was that it took me a long time and a roundabout route to get the opportunity to play for the club. Some of it was, I suppose, my own fault because I did not work hard enough when I began playing at Boys' Club level. And, inevitably, I found myself in trouble when I was just a kid and I chucked playing the game when I was 13 after I had been suspended. I was sent off two weeks in succession when I was playing for Aberdeen Boys' Club and when that happened I just thought I had had enough and walked away from the game. The lads who ran the club in Glasgow were Robert Calderwood and

Jimmy Connor and they looked after me. They persuaded me to play again and Aberdeen signed me on an S Form and while it wasn't Rangers it was a top senior side who wanted me. Joe Miller was an S Form signing at the same time as I was and so was Steve Gray who played for Aberdeen and then Airdrie. We used to go up to Pittodrie during the holidays. We trained there and the club monitored our progress every summer and every Easter when we were off school.

Of course, Alex Ferguson was the manager then and Archie Knox was his assistant and years later I was to work under Archie at Ibrox when he was No.2 to Walter Smith. Really, though, we did not see too much of them. They were working with the first-team players, with John Hewitt and Willie Miller, Alex McLeish, Gordon Strachan and Stewart Kennedy. They were the stars up there then and it was an amazing array of talent Fergie brought together. Not too long after the times I went up there these players were to go on to win the Cup-Winners' Cup but, by the time that happened I had been kicked out. When I was 16 Alex Ferguson called me into his office and told me that the coaching staff didn't think I was going to make it. He said I was too small and that I wasn't strong enough. He was very good about it and while I was shattered I knew that what he was saying was right. At the time I was small and it was only after I started to work – because now I had to get some kind of job quickly because football didn't seem to be an option for me – that I took a stretch and filled out a bit. When he let me go, though, he was doing the right thing. It dented what ambitions I had about being a footballer but it didn't stop me playing. I went back to the Boy's Club in Glasgow and then I started to get a game for the works team. I was a van boy with a lemonade company in the East End of Glasgow, Dunn and Moore, and eventually I worked there for three years. Anyhow, you know how it is, when there was a break a kick-about would start and from these little games I was handed the chance of playing for the works side. I had to get stronger and fitter to handle the job and so, while I was playing against lads much older than I was, it was something that I could handle now. To be honest, I had given up on the idea of being a professional and I accepted the offer of playing just to have a bit of fun because I didn't see the point in becoming too serious about the game any more. Funnily enough it was then, when I wasn't too worried, that I got my first real break in the game – the one which was to give me the chance of playing full-time. And the chance, too, of joining Rangers, something which seemed out of my reach back then. The man who ran the team thought I had the makings of something better and he went to see the owner of the company, Joseph Dunn.

The result was that Mr Dunn came to watch me and, afterwards, he invited me to his office and asked if I would like to train with Clyde, the club which had always been owned by his family. Following on from that I played for Clyde in a few youth games, one against Celtic, and I was offered a contract with them. The Aberdeen deal had gone wrong but that made no difference to the way I was thinking. This was a chance and I recognised it as such and nothing could have dissuaded me from trying my luck with a senior club once more.

Obviously going to Shawfield was a whole lot different from being at Pittodrie. This was a small club without the glamour which Aberdeen possessed back then and also without the star players who were always around when I went up there for these weeks of training. Yet I did not miss any of that. This change came at the right time for me and I am convinced to this day that joining Clyde when I did was a key factor in how I turned out as a player. The entire set-up was light years away from the one which Alex Ferguson had at Aberdeen but it was what I required. The manager was Craig Brown, who would soon go on to join Scotland's international team as assistant to Andy Roxburgh to begin with and then as manager in his own right. He was brilliant with the young players and the experienced lads who were in the Clyde first team then and was just as good at putting in time with the youths or reserves. There were guys such as Paul Flexney, Brian Ahern and Steve Evans and I learned a lot from them. All of them wanted to help youngsters such as myself who were starting out in the game. So you were getting encouragement from them and from Craig Brown and I'll always be grateful for my spell there. To some extent Craig seemed to take me under his wing a little bit, possibly because I was one of the youngest players at the club, and I cannot say a bad word about that man. All you heard at Shawfield was encouragement and when you are a kid that is music to your ears.

Ultimately I had only a couple of seasons or so with Clyde but that was the major learning ground for me and when I moved on it was to St Mirren and even now I look back and think how bizarre that transfer was. Clearly my allegiances were still with Rangers as far as support went, nothing can ever alter that. Yet when my first major transfer book took place – and £65,000 was a lot of money for St Mirren to pay Clyde at that time – it happened at Ibrox just after I had played in an Under-21 game there for Scotland. It was really strange. There I was at Ibrox at last, signing new forms just as I had always wanted to do, except, of course, I was not joining Rangers. Instead Alex Miller was taking me to Love Street and I was signing quite happily because going to Rangers still appeared an impossible dream and this was an opportunity to play full-time and that had an enormous appeal. It was something that I had always wanted to become, after all, a full-time professional and after the Aberdeen set-back I was now making the grade. This was a major career move for me but what I didn't know is that Rangers had been interested enough to send a scout to watch me. Years later Walter Smith told me that he had heard good reports, asked a scout to take in a couple of Clyde games and the report came back that I was "not what Rangers were looking for". Shades of Aberdeen! And in more ways than one – because later Rangers did sign me, paying a dozen times or more what Clyde had been looking for, and Alex Ferguson also tried to take me to Old Trafford. As Jimmy Greaves says, it's a funny old game right enough.

It was another couple of years before I reached Rangers and even then it was in one of the most long drawn-out transfer sagas I had ever known and it seemed all the longer because I was at the centre of it and there were occasions when I know I placed my whole career in danger because I was so determined to get my own way when I knew that Rangers wanted me and had offered very close to £1 million to sign me.

The season after winning the Scottish Cup with St Mirren – I scored the only goal in the Final at Hampden against Dundee United in 1987 – I signed a new contract with the Paisley club where Alex Smith was now the manager. Again he was a man who encouraged me and someone who gave me a lot of help and a whole lot of sound advice. On this occasion, though, I was not for listening even to his words of wisdom. To be fair, Alex was the voice of reason in the whole affair and I behaved badly. I was young and I thought the chance of playing for Rangers might be denied me.

I was torn at the time between a loyalty to Alex Smith and achieving what was my major ambition in the game and while I felt that there were times when I was kicking Alex in the teeth I could not help myself. I'm not proud of my behaviour at that period because I know now that I was being really unreasonable and ignoring the fact that Alex Smith had been good to me, that St Mirren had given me my first full-time breakthrough and that it was only a matter of months since I had signed a new contract with the club. Back then, though, nothing mattered to me more than getting to Ibrox. I was so scared that I would miss the opportunity, that Graeme Souness, who was the Rangers manager at the time, would give up if St Mirren continued to refuse to sell me. The story had broken in the newspapers that Graeme wanted me and since the very early days of the Ibrox revolution he had masterminded there had not been many occasions when he had been unsuccessful in the transfer market. It was also well known that when Graeme was looking to sign a player, he was always ready to pay top dollar to get him. Still, while that heartened me a little there was a wee thought lurking at the back of my mind that if St Mirren continued to say "NO" then he could go out and buy someone else for the position.

And so I took to haunting the manager's office, morning and afternoon I would be knocking on his door and asking if there had been any developments, if there had been an official bid from Rangers, if there had even been an enquiry and Alex would straight-bat me as he had to do because his job was always to act in the best interest of St Mirren. He was smart enough to know what was going through my mind. There had never been any secret about the team I supported, and the club I would like to play for above all others, and so he recognised that as long as the stories persisted then my mind was going to be in turmoil. During it all – and it lasted something like a couple of months – he tried to talk sense into me. When we talked he was always supportive but trying to point out to me that I could not continue to make trouble at the club, which is what I was doing in some ways. Basically, I felt that if I made a nuisance of myself then St Mirren's directors would cave in and sell me because they needed the money just as every other provincial club needed cash.

I wasn't training with the other first-team players and when I was involved in games my form was terrible. Now, a lot of people thought that I just was not trying, but that wasn't the case. What was wrong with me was that the entire business had got on top of me. I couldn't sleep right, couldn't train properly, couldn't think about anything else but the possibility that I would be sold to Rangers and so my game, like the rest of my life, had gone to pieces.

Now Alex Smith wanted to keep me. He honestly felt that if he could keep together the team which had won the Cup then St Mirren would become a stronger side in the seasons ahead. At the same time he had laboured long and hard in the lower reaches of the Scottish games and he knew better than anyone just how much the smaller Scottish clubs relied on transfer money to keep them alive. He probably realised before the directors did that eventually I would have to be sold if my heart was not in playing for the club any longer. Yet he refused to allow that fact to surface in his talks with me. He was always trying to convince me to stay on, to honour my contract and then, he pointed out, I would still be young enough to make a move to a bigger club if that was the route I wanted to take. He was terrific about the whole thing even though I gave him a fresh headache just about every day.

There was a point when I was ready to walk out on the club altogether and risk my entire career. It had reached that stage with me. It was almost as if I had come to some kind of breaking point and I would have done that and taken the consequences rather than sit around and watch my hopes of playing for Rangers vanish without putting up any kind of fight. The first indication that the directors had changed tack came when Alex Smith called me into his office and told me that Alex Ferguson had been in touch from Manchester United and the two clubs had more or less agreed on a fee and that he thought I should consider this opportunity. I even spoke to Alex Ferguson on the phone but I explained to him how I felt and said that while I understood just how great the offer of going to Old Trafford was my heart would not be in it and he understood. I told Alex Smith the same and then my old manager from Clyde spoke to me. Craig Brown was now in charge of the Scotland Under-21 team and he spoke to me and his advice was to go south.

He felt that I should accept the offer from Manchester United and, then, if I wanted to return from England after a few years then I could fulfil my ambition of being a Rangers player. I listened to Craig because I valued his advice, I knew that it was well-intentioned, but even as he spoke I knew that I would not follow the path he was suggesting. Actually the talk with Craig led to a fall-out between him and Graeme Souness, though I knew that Craig was simply trying to guide me towards what he thought quite genuinely was going to be in my best interests. Graeme took a different view though it was all sorted later.

Anyhow, I knew then that the transfer would come and while St Mirren were, as far as I am aware, ready to accept just half a million pounds from Manchester United they added a premium to the price when they decided, reluctantly, to sell me to Ibrox. Rangers had to fork out around £850,000 to sign me and that meant that St Mirren had made a profit of almost £800,000 in a couple of seasons. When I left I didn't see that they had too much to complain about!

As for myself, I had what I had always wanted but I have to say the weight of that transfer fee was a burden when I first arrived at the club. When Graeme kicked off the Rangers revolution just a little over two years before, he had signed Terry Butcher, then England's international team captain, for three-quarters of a million pounds. Now here was I, with only a handful of Under-21 caps to my name, costing more than that. Even allowing for the escalation in the cost of players it seemed outrageous to me that I should have been sold for that much money. I felt weighed down by the price which had been put on my head. It's easy to turn round and say that the value has nothing to do with you – nor does it – but it can still affect you and it did me. I signed for the club on February 15, 1988 and 12 days later I made my debut in a game away from home against Dundee United at Tannadice. In between times I had suffered as a fan as the team went out of the Scottish Cup to Dunfermline only days after I joined up. There had not been too long a time available for me to settle in and become used to being among all these big-name players but Graeme had decided that I should start my first-team career as soon as possible and after being ineligible for the Cup, this was it.

So there I was in a Rangers team which read: Woods, Nicholl, Bartram, Roberts, Wilkins, Gough, Derek Ferguson, myself, Nisbet, Durrant and Walters. It was Mark Walters who scored the goal but this was not to be the best season to come to Ibrox. After the initial year when Graeme Souness and Walter Smith took over they had won the League Cup and also the Championship. When I arrived they had won the League Cup again, but before I kicked a ball they were out of the Scottish Cup and eventually they lost the League to Celtic as well and I was in the team which plunged to defeat in the last Old Firm game of the season. It was at Ibrox and Celtic won 2-1 with Jan Bartram scoring our goal but it was not enough, and never going to be enough. It was a difficult time to slot into the side and we lost four of the eight games I played in at the end of that year. I scored one goal in an away game against Morton – and we lost that one 3-2 incidentally – and Rangers finished in third place. That was the lowest League placing I was to know in all the years which lay ahead … I did not know that at the time, however, and so it was hard to take after the bright beginning the club had had under the new management team the previous season. Everyone had expected that to continue and it was a major disappointment when it didn't happen, particularly for a new boy who was trying to find his feet like myself.

Thankfully I had no inkling of what was in store for me on a personal basis as I relaxed that close season and looked forward to kicking off the new term with Rangers on a quest for the title which had been lost to our oldest rivals. I contented myself with thinking that the trophy was only out on loan and that was to be proved right. But while the team simply won more and more trophies as the seasons went by I had my own devils to battle. And there were times when even the medals could not make up for the heartbreak I was feeling as my form slumped and so many of the fans turned against me. It was the worst period of my life and it went on for something like 18 months. Something was wrong with me and I did not know what it was. Nor did any of the training staff, nor the doctors. But I knew that I was ill in some way. I had no stamina, no strength, no real desire to play the game at all, though Graeme kept persisting with me as a member of the first-team squad.

Looking back I am sure that Graeme simply felt that this was something I could play my way through. That if I continued to train as normal, and play in the team then eventually everything would turn out to be okay. Sadly, for me, that was not the case and the problem dragged on and on and there were times I feared that I might be forced to give up the game. Not too long before, the Celtic winger, Davie Provan, had been forced to retire suffering from ME after a long period when he, too, had not known exactly what was wrong with him. Little wonder that Davie's situation kept pushing its way into my thoughts as the doctors could not determine what was happening to me. It became the worst period of my life and I was not helped by the booing I had to endure from the Rangers supporters – these same supporters I used to stand beside on the terracing. That was the lowest point of my entire career, worse than being turned down by Aberdeen, worse than having to go to work in the lemonade factory and trying to forget about football as a career, worse than the two months when St Mirren were refusing to sell me, because I felt that I was being rejected by my own people. And that hurt deeply. There were occasions when I went home in tears, literally crying through a combination of frustration at not knowing what was wrong and hurt at the jeers I was hearing whenever I touched the ball. I don't blame the Rangers fans now. They were in the dark just as I was. They did not realise that there was something wrong with me and, to be honest, I just wish Graeme Souness had perhaps spoken out a little more about the worries which surrounded my fitness. Perhaps he was trying to protect me, believing it was simply a form slump which would end as quickly and mysteriously as it had arrived. Of course, as well as the general fitness levels being lower than usual, I also found myself more and more susceptible to injuries. There was a knock-on effect and all that did was further depress me and that did not exactly help matters either. You know, it sounds crazy now, but on one occasion I was injured and sitting in the stand watching Rangers play and a ball went to Gary Stevens and he made a bad pass or he didn't clear the ball properly and the guy sitting next to me started to give him stick. Only he wasn't handing out the verbals to Gary – I was his target! He had seen a mistake and the fair hair and it was enough.

He hadn't seen the teams and he hadn't looked around him when he sat down and when I jarred him you should have seen the look on his face. He couldn't believe it. He had convinced himself that I was playing and that any error was going to be mine and he had his mind set when he went to the game and it only changed when he realised that I was sitting there. When I asked him "What do you think you are talking about pal?" he did not know where to look. He babbled out an apology but, in a way, he did me a favour because I realised there and then that some of the supporters were going to be on my back whether I was doing well or badly, whether, indeed, I was even in the team or not. There was no logic to their behaviour at times and that gave me a little comfort. It helped place things in perspective although, of course, the booing continued whenever I played until eventually the doctors found out what they thought was wrong.

It was such a simple thing that, initially, I could not believe what they were telling me. Essentially the diagnosis was that I was suffering from a blood disorder which was stemming from my tonsils and they recommended that my tonsils should be removed and I underwent that minor operation and, amazingly, everything changed for the better. After the tonsils were removed I felt wonderful, better than I had done in years. The poison had been going through my blood stream and affecting my entire system. That was why I had felt so weak, why I couldn't raise any energy at training or during games. I just couldn't believe that it had been something so simple which had come so close to wrecking my career with Rangers. For, believe me, that was what was happening. I was so depressed by everything that all the various side-effects were magnified in my mind. Each injury seemed worse than the one before. Each time I was jeered it was harder to accept. Each time I was substituted I felt that Rangers were rejecting me. That was not the case. Graeme and Walter had always kept faith with me and while their belief in my ability might have been tested during these seasons it was never destroyed. They saw something that was not so apparent to some of the fans and they persisted in playing me and over the years since I would like to think that I have been able to pay them back and the club, too. It would have broken my heart if they had decided to sell me.

There were occasions when Walter called me into his office and told me that there were clubs interested in buying me but I was never sure if he was testing me, or even winding me up, because he knew that there was no way I would ever have wanted to leave Ibrox. There was interest from Wolves at one stage and then there were newspaper reports that Alex Miller wanted to take me to Aberdeen when he was the manager at Pittodrie. I didn't hear anything official at all about that one and I am still with the club, still at the only place I have ever wanted to play my football. If the day comes when it all ends and I am told that Rangers don't want me any more then obviously I would have to think about another club. But if that happens then I would leave with a heavy heart because part of me would always be at Ibrox. Having said that, Ally McCoist and Ian Durrant and Andy Goram have proved that there is life after Rangers. These three players were like me, they would probably have wanted to end their careers with the club they had supported for so long, the club which had brought them too many good times and so much success. Yet they have gone on to carve out new football lives for themselves and both Durrant and Coisty have been selected for Scotland again since they moved to Kilmarnock. They have also helped the Rugby Park team to stay near the top of the Scottish Premier League.

The Goalie, too, after a few miserable months has signed a contract with Motherwell and has helped them stay in the Top 10 and has also been praised by the Scotland manager, Craig Brown. So, while the thought of leaving Rangers is not something that I like to dwell upon for any length of time, the examples are out there demonstrating that life does go on. I suppose we all know that nothing will ever equal the nine or 10 years we were all together winning medals almost every single season and making history for the club as the years went by. No one can ever take these memories away and that is why it was so important to me that I did achieve my goal. That I was able to sign for Rangers when so many barriers were being placed in my path. That I came through the agonies of that "mystery" illness and won back the support for the fans and that, finally, the club awarded me a Testimonial after I had completed 11 years at Ibrox. It seems so long ago since I made my debut in a season which turned out to be so painful for everyone concerned with Rangers. Okay, the League Cup had been won in a penalty shoot-out with Aberdeen after a 3-3 draw at Hampden but from then on it was all downhill. A few days after I signed – even before I played that first game – the team lost to Dunfermline in the Scottish Cup at East End Park. The following month we went out of the European Cup against Steaua Bucharest on a 3-2 aggregate and again I was a spectator as I had not been signed before the quarter-final deadline. And, of course, we finished up third in the League as Celtic won the title.

However, agony breeds determination. What followed was a decade of unrelenting success for the club, one which allowed someone such as myself who had grown up in the East End of Glasgow to claim 10 League Championship medals, three Scottish Cup medals and five League Cup badges. As a schoolboy going to support the team, I would never have believed that would happen. As a lemonade van boy after being rejected by Aberdeen I would have laughed if you had even suggested I would be playing for Rangers, far less celebrating so many victories. That, though, is what makes football the great game that it is. Success can be grasped by anyone if they work hard enough and if they are lucky enough to get a few breaks at the right time. Mine came when I was seen playing for the works team and then given the chance by Craig Brown to play for Clyde. That's where it all began …

3

CHAPTER THREE

The Mad, Mad World of Paolo Di Canio

The way I have always approached the game it is always a reasonable bet that somewhere along the way I shall find myself in trouble on the field. I have always played hard but I think that most opposing players would agree that while I can hand out knocks during games, in the same way, I can accept a few kicks without squealing about it.

In Scotland it has always been a man's game, after all, and you like to believe that a mutual respect can exist among fellow professionals. Take, for example, two of the Celtic players I faced up to regularly over the years in dozens of Old Firm games, Peter Grant and Paul McStay. In my book they were both tremendous professionals and, equally, they were out-and-out Celtic men. That added to the respect I had for them. In effect it was a mirror image of myself – these two players had the same feelings for Celtic, for their club, as I had for Rangers, which was my club. I like to think that they had the same feelings towards me even though we might have had the odd difference or two in the heat of the battle.

I was with these two lads in Scotland teams at Under-21 and full international level and there was never a single problem between us on these occasions. Indeed, Granty and myself went back to when I was playing for Clyde and winning my first Under-21 honour. He never hid his feelings for Celtic and when I joined Rangers I was the same. We wore our hearts on our sleeves I suppose but I saw nothing wrong with that. And I still don't see anything wrong with it when the players involved are sincere. It would have been worse to try to hide it because that would mean being less than honest. I know how Peter Grant must have felt during the period when we were dominating the domestic game. I hadn't much liked it when Celtic were on top and I was just a supporter then so it must have hurt him deeply to be involved and I could feel for him. Okay, I was enjoying myself as a Rangers player but you could still find time to think how it must have felt for someone in the opposing team and Granty was the one who must have been suffering most.

Anyhow, I think you would understand from the foregoing that I have absolutely no problems with Celtic players who are professional and who are genuine in their beliefs. And I would carry that attitude on right through all the teams I have faced in my career. Sure, there have been a few scrapes here and there – including one with Paul Gascoigne which I'll return to – but the highly-publicised row with Paolo Di Canio was a different matter altogether. It was the nastiest incident I have ever been dragged into and the Italian is a player I dislike intensely. He is a liar and he is a coward and I would tell him that if ever he is man enough to face me. Of course, I know that he is not man enough, in fact, I don't consider him much of a man at all after the way he behaved in an explosive Old Firm game at Celtic Park when we were on our way to winning the ninth League Championship in succession. It was not the kind of make-or-break situation which we witnessed last season when the title was actually decided at Parkhead and when Rangers made history by lifting the Championship right there in the home of our greatest rivals.

That season we had been beaten by Celtic in the fifth round of the Scottish Cup in a game which took place just 10 days before the last Old Firm League match of the season. We had injury worries – something which was inevitable during the years as the demands on the players became greater and greater. The Gaffer (Walter Smith) brought back Mark Hateley for the game and we were forced to play third choice on-loan goalkeeper Andy Dibble in place of Andy Goram who was injured and Theo Snelders who went out of the team at the last minute.

Everything was stacked against us and yet the return of big Mark helped to lift the players, and the supporters and it had an intimidating effect on the Celtic defence as he powered himself into aerial challenges which he won with astonishing regularity.

When Brian Laudrup scored I think we all knew that we were going to win the game and while there was a handful of games left I also think we knew that we were going to win the historic Championship.

It was then, in the second half of the game, and again at the end, that Paolo Di Canio decided that he wanted to take revenge on me for the result which had gone against Celtic. He clearly threatened me and even jostled me as he tried to provoke me.

The hand gestures he indulged in made it fairly clear that he intended to do one of two things, either he wanted to snap one of my legs or he wanted to wring my neck. I walked away from trouble the first time and then, when his histrionics continued at the end in front of 50,000 people I just said to him "Up the tunnel, just you and me" and he vanished. There was not the slightest chance that I was going to let him drag me into trouble and maybe spark off trouble in the stands when we had already seen two players, Mark Hateley and Malky Mackay, red-carded in a second-half flare-up. Nor was I wanting to embarrass myself or my club by getting involved in a brawl where everyone could see us and which millions of television viewers would be able to watch in their living rooms. That's why I was happy to ask him to see me out of sight of the mass audience and then sort out the problem man to man. It was not the right thing to do, probably just slightly more sensible than scrapping in plain sight of everyone. But I was provoked and I was angry that this guy should suddenly be having a go at me for no reason other than that his team had lost.

There had been nothing to cause this kind of hysteria. There had been a spat or two during the game and the occasional one in other matches but always these had ended with his mouth music and me walking away from him. This time he had gone too far and I felt myself become more and more angry when I got to the dressing room. Alex Cleland and Craig Moore had heard me speak to Di Canio as the teams were getting ready to leave the field. They had tried to calm me down and some of the other lads were also doing their bit to make sure that I would come to my senses and forget all about it. That's what I should have done. Instead once I had been in the bath and then got dressed I went to the Players' Lounge looking for Di Canio and looking for what I thought would be justice after his antics on the field. I did want to sort it out, to hear him apologise maybe, because he had threatened me in front of the players and in front of all those people watching the game and that rankled. But he wasn't there. He was the only Celtic player who wasn't there. I spoke to one or two of their lads and Tom Boyd told me to forget about it and everyone was fine but Paolo Di Canio did not turn up. That's one of the reasons I have no respect for him as a man.

He knew that I would be looking for him, I had told him that at the end of the game. He knew where I would be. So there were two things for him to do as far as I was concerned – he could come along, shake hands and apologise and end the whole silly business. Or he could say that he wanted to have a go at me again and we would have had to sort that out. He chose a third way. The coward's way. He vanished into the night and to compound his actions he gave interviews to some of the tabloid newspapers the following day where he accused me of insulting him during the game and calling him names which were derogatory to his religion. I was alerted to this latest problem by a journalist who called me and asked for my reaction. To be fair he could not have printed it because I went ballistic. Here was the guy who could not face me the night before still going behind my back in an effort to land me in bother.

It was vicious and it was uncalled for and it was utterly malicious and without the slightest grain of truth. It was then that I did something which I had never done before and which, thank God, I have never had to do since. I lifted the telephone and dialled the number for Celtic Park and asked if I could speak to their manager, Tommy Burns.

Looking back after the event I don't know how I was able to do that because it was a real breach of football protocol. Players just don't go about phoning up opposition managers to air their grievances especially when surrounded by the inflammatory after-match atmosphere of an Old Firm game. The only way I can explain it is that I felt I had to do something to stop all of this and I thought that Tommy Burns would be the type of person who would listen to me. Again, we are back to someone who is committed to his own cause. As a player and then as the club's manager Tommy was one thousand per cent Celtic and, as I have explained, I have no problems with that. Any problems I do have are with those players such as Di Canio who soft-soap supporters into thinking that they are dedicated to the one club and then walk off to another team and give their fans the same run-around as they sign yet another lucrative contract!

That day I was put through to Tommy who must have been a bit startled to hear me on the phone to him but I have to say that if he was surprised or even shocked he behaved like a gentleman.

That was no more than I expected but the hearing he gave me went beyond my expectations and heightened the regard I had always had for him as a man. I appreciated that as a manager he had to stand by his own player in public but when I told him that I had not said any of the things I was accused of saying he accepted my word. I told him that I would swear on my family's lives that I had never insulted him in any remotely religious manner. Then I said to him that I would drive to Celtic Park that very minute and if he got Di Canio there I would go into a room with the two of them and tell him to his face that he was a liar and then watch his reaction. Of course, I realise now that was something that was never going to happen but Tommy listened to me and he seemed to understand that I was absolutely honest and sincere in what I was saying to him. Eventually we began to talk about the game and he was very complimentary to me and that meant a lot when you consider the emotional state I was in by this stage of the proceedings.

The point which escaped me at the time because I was so obsessed with my own little feud with Di Canio was that Tommy must have been in a little bit of a state himself. He must have known that he had just lost the title again and that meant the record nine-in-a-row sequence of championship victories which Celtic had guarded so proudly had now been lost. Yet, as the complete professional he has always been, he heard me out and then found time to encourage me. He could have hung up on me right away. He could have just refused to take the call altogether. Or he could have told me that he would report me to my club for calling him in that way. Any of these actions would have been understandable in the circumstances we both found ourselves in. It was not an easy thing for Tommy to speak to me and yet he did it and I shall always value the time I spent with him on the telephone that day. It was a side of the Old Firm rivalry that more of the supporters should recognise. Di Canio apart, I cannot remember having any off-field problems with Celtic players in more than 10 years of taking part in these matches.

The fact that Tommy Burns gave me his time in that manner is as big a compliment as any I have ever been paid in my career. No doubt there will be supporters out there who won't believe me.

There will be some, too, who just don't want to believe it because there is a popular misconception that Old Firm players do not get on with each other off the field. That is a myth. There is a mutual respect between players which does not allow that to happen when we do get together on international occasions. It would be better for the games and the atmosphere which surrounds the games if more of the fans were to realise that.

To return to Di Canio for a moment, it was no surprise to me when he became embroiled in the incident with referee Paul Alcock while he was at Sheffield Wednesday. It was the biggest certainty in the world that he would get himself in trouble with the authorities in England. That is, after all, what he does best! Predictably he was able to throw himself into an incident which had not had anything to do with him initially. Then he knocks referee Alcock to the ground and afterwards, again predictably, he blamed the official. I knew exactly how that poor man felt because it followed the same pattern as with me. Cause the bother, play the supposed hero for your team's supporters, and then when the trouble becomes a little bit serious blame someone else. Then, of course, he just walked out on another of the clubs he "loved" and is happily proclaiming his new allegiance to West Ham and so it will continue.

Oh, he does, of course, still allow his opinion on matters Celtic to be aired and I had to laugh when he weighed in with his views on Hugh Dallas and the troubled Old Firm game at the end of last season. It helps to keep him popular with some of the Celtic supporters I suppose but it doesn't kid me and I don't suppose it will kid too many of his former team-mates as we all wait to see which team badge he will be kissing next. He gave me a very difficult time and his attitude afterwards was totally unrepentant and therefore don't expect me to forgive him ever. As far as I'm concerned he just doesn't exist.

I had a much worse run-in on the field with Paul Gascoigne, some of you may remember – and yet when he joined up at Rangers we were able to talk about it and shake hands and put the whole thing behind us. As professionals usually do.

Gazza was with Spurs when we tangled in a pre-season friendly at Ibrox soon after he had signed for the London club. He was being hailed then as the new star of English football and Graeme Souness, who was still managing Rangers at the time, decided that I was the player he wanted to man-mark him. It was a job Graeme often handed to me and it was one which brought with it a certain amount of hassle. No creative player likes to have someone going with him everywhere on the field, simply having been delegated to STOP him playing rather than being asked to do anything himself. It is frustrating and it leads to outbursts from the victims of the marking. I don't think I have seen any player take kindly to the tactic. Some can defeat it. Others can't and that's when you get the type of flare-up which had Gazza and yours truly literally spitting their anger at each other. Of course, I reckon that he believed that he was coming up to Glasgow for a little stroll around in the sun without the game being played at any great competitive level. What he didn't understand was that Rangers don't play "friendlies" in that sense, that the supporters would not allow any of the players to take it easy against English opposition and, lastly, that Graeme just didn't like to lose to anyone. At anything.

So there I was snapping at his heels from the start of the game and he didn't like it one little bit and, of course, he wasn't meant to. Then he spat at me and I snapped. I spat back at him at one stage – something I am not proud of doing even though it was done in retaliation – and eventually I was running around the pitch after him like a bull in a china shop. The mist came down and he made it worse by giving me a few verbals and finally Graeme took me off before I was sent off. But, while it was bad at the time, there were no grudges. I didn't hold it against Gazza when he came to Rangers and he took the same attitude. We had a laugh about it after he had signed and the whole silly business was hardly ever talked about again after his first day. That is the way it should be. Every player can be out of order on the field at times but that shouldn't drag on. It never did with Peter Grant or Paul McStay when I played against them. The residue of ill will only come with one person – Paolo Di Canio – and I can never forget the troubles he put me through.

4

CHAPTER FOUR

The Souness Revolution and Beyond

The man who signed me for Rangers and, in effect opened the way to the success which followed, was, of course, Graeme Souness and I arrived at Ibrox just as the revolution he had kicked off was gathering pace.

It was an exciting place to be, demanding of course because Graeme was not a manager who would happily settle for second best and he let you know that in no uncertain terms. In fact, he would underline that message on a daily basis if he felt that was required. In his first season he had suffered disappointment only in the Scottish Cup. The two other domestic trophies, the League Cup and the Championship, had been won and the fans who had been deserting the club were back in their thousands recognising that in Souness, Rangers might have found the manager who would turn the club round in the same way as Jock Stein had done with Celtic 20 years earlier. I know I felt that when I looked on from the outside, still a St Mirren player of course, but watching carefully what was happening at Rangers.

The impact Souness had on the entire Scottish game was enormous. The players at Ibrox saw it at first hand but at every other club we looked on in amazement as top English international players turned their backs on the game down south and joined up at Ibrox. Prior to Souness that would never have happened. He was responsible for persuading Terry Butcher, then the England captain and just back from the World Cup in Mexico, to reject a signing offer from Manchester United and move to Scotland instead. Chris Woods, too, came north and others followed and suddenly Rangers had become a powerful, all-British force rather than the big fish the club had always been in the small pond of

Scottish football. It was quite extraordinary and a lot of us looking on as spectators could not quite grasp what was suddenly going on. The whole business has been described since as a revolution and that is exactly how it felt. It was as if the game in Scotland which had gone trundling along on its own for more than a century would never quite be the same again. Rangers fans, naturally, loved every minute of it but Souness was not looked on kindly by the game's establishment.

He was abrasive, of course, and there was a kind of arrogance about him on occasions and that rubbed people up the wrong way. He was also very single minded and could be absolutely ruthless when that was required of him. When I signed – after all the transfer hassles I suffered and mentioned earlier – I have to admit I was more than a little in awe of the man. Obviously he had impressed me as a player with Liverpool and with Scotland and had still shown, as player-manager, tremendous skill and vision on the field during his first season. Following that initial period his appearances dropped off but on the training ground there were few signs that his abilities had withered very much.

Then there was the manner in which he had swept into his first job as a manager, taking to the task as if he had been born to boss a football team. And there was his presence. Graeme was a very impressive man and when I was signing on as a young player that struck me very forcibly. It didn't matter how big the reputations of players who were in that dressing room at the time were, when Graeme Souness walked in, he was The Boss. No one could think anything other than that. It was just the way he was. He was a hard, hard man but I have to say that I enjoyed the years I spent playing under his guidance. From the very beginning I learned that you had to show him respect and that if you failed to do that then your career was not going to last too long. In fact, you were finished.

Also if you went behind his back about anything at all then you would be as well just to pack your boots and start to look for another club. Because if you crossed Graeme then you were not going to be forgiven. It was his way or no way. Now that may sound wrong to people who have never experienced what it is like to play the game at a professional level. It isn't, though, that's the way managers have to be if they are going to be successful. They might go about things in different ways – but they have to be in charge and everyone from the top player at the club to the youngest apprentice has to realise that. Some managers will be less confrontational than others but talking or walking around a situation was never Graeme's way. He met every problem head on, any challenge which came up was met in the same way, and you knew if you happened to find yourself on the receiving end of one of his notorious blasts.

He was never exactly the kind of manager you talked with about a game immediately after the final whistle. If you had been hammered for a mistake or what he might have thought was lack of effort, then to answer back when the heat of battle was still in the air was absolutely the wrong thing to do. It was always better to wait until the Monday morning and then ask to see him and put your point and hope that he would take your viewpoint into consideration. You were usually able to talk calmly then – though not always, because Graeme was a fairly explosive individual. Nor was he a respecter of reputations. It didn't matter much to him if the player who had stepped out of line was a major star at club and international level or one who had cost a great deal of money or if he was the newest kid on the block, they were all treated the same. If you made the mistake of arguing with the Gaffer in public then you had to be prepared to take the consequences.

I am sure that you all remember Graham Roberts and what happened to him, and he was a hero with the fans at the time he had his rather spectacular fall-out with Graeme. It was my first season there and it had not been the best for the club with just the League Cup in the Trophy Room and after the second-last match of the season, which we lost 1-0 to Aberdeen, Graham Roberts seemed to decide that he was going to face down the manager after he had been blamed for losing that goal. He refused to accept the blame and right there in the dressing room he started to argue with Graeme and then Walter Smith, who was the assistant manager back then, and we were all sitting there knowing in our hearts how this was all going to end. There was only one winner but Robbo, experienced professional that he was, did not seem able to get that into his head. I still don't know what got into him that day. Maybe he thought that because he was such a major favourite with the fans that he would be bullet proof. Maybe he thought that he would escape any retribution because he had been a key player with the club ever since signing from Spurs. Whatever it was, he under-estimated Graeme Souness. The following week when he was dropped from the first team he turned up at Falkirk's ground, Brockville, and sat among the fans in the stand and was given a hero's welcome. When that happened I think all the lads knew he had signed his own death warrant. We knew his career had ended. And that's how it turned out. At the start of the next season Graham was training with the reserves. He was sent to play for the third team at the most obscure venues and very soon he had been sold on and Graeme Souness had made his point. Very, very forcibly! Essentially that was one of his great strengths as a manager. He had that ruthless streak that the best of managers always possess – he used to say that Bob Paisley had been utterly ruthless at Liverpool in his dealings with players – and he was focussed always on winning. Whether the victories he aimed for were on or off the field they were pursued with the same vigour. It was that trait which made him such a special and influential player and it also played a huge role in his managerial spells. He demanded a great deal from the team, from every individual player, but you knew that he would never make demands on you that he wouldn't make on himself.

That is why he commanded such respect in the dressing room because we also knew that he would stand by his players at all times if they had been honest with him. If you misled him, or showed him anything other than respect, then it was over. Actually, while the flashpoint for Robbo was the dressing room row after the Aberdeen game with its subsequent Falkirk fall-out, I had sensed that something might happen between the two of them. There had been a little bit of friction over the previous week or two between them, mainly I suppose because the results had not been as good as Graeme had wanted. It might have been that he thought Robbo was getting a bit too big for his boots and that if an example had to be made before the start of the next League campaign then he might be the one and, of course, once Robbo began to dispute his role in the loss of that goal against Aberdeen that was it. Robbo should have known better because when that type of post-mortem was taking place following a defeat Graeme could be a fearsome sight. If he thought players were cheating on him, or if someone had not been following the pre-match instruction and had lost a goal because of that then you could expect fireworks at half-time or after the match was over. He was never one to miss and hit the wall. If you were going to get it then there was not much you could do.

We have all heard the stories of Alex Ferguson hurling tea cups around the dressing room. That was nothing! When Graeme flew into one of his tantrums nothing was safe. Doors would be booted in. Hampers would be kicked around. A television set was wrecked one day and, really, anything that came to hand was liable to be smashed against a wall. It was a sight to behold. Later, when Graeme had gone to Liverpool, Walter would sometimes do the same. But he never reached the level of Graeme's explosions. Nor did he throw a wobbly as often. It was a regular occurrence with Graeme. When he wanted to get a point over then he would do it with any weapons which were at hand and with which he felt he could underline his anger.

Since he left there have been stories of him becoming involved while he was with Galatasaray in Turkey and with Benfica in Portugal. Rows with supporters, battles with opposing players, and here I was sitting back home thinking that by now he would have mellowed after the years of experience he has racked up. I did believe that he would have become a little wiser, a bit more restrained and yet the passion he brought with him to Rangers is still there and the flames are always ready to be lit. I suppose it's that attitude which helped him stand out as a leader on the field and a very inspirational manager off the field when he stepped into the Ibrox hotseat. As far as I'm concerned you cannot praise Graeme Souness highly enough. Not just because of what he achieved at Rangers but what he also did to enliven the entire Scottish game. The Ibrox revolution would not have happened without him. He arrived in Glasgow, recognised straight away that here was a sleeping giant and gave the club the rudest awakening it has ever had. He took on all the other clubs who had been successful during Rangers' dark days. He stood up against Celtic and Aberdeen and Dundee United who had enjoyed their years in the sunshine and were determined that Rangers would not grow to be powerful again. He had to stand up to them all, face the opposition which was there and the jealousy he himself aroused and get on with the job. Not an easy job either, one which had defeated Jock Wallace when he had returned a couple of years earlier in an effort then to breathe fresh life into Rangers. It is hard to put into words what all of this meant to the players and to the supporters. Rangers had been too long in the shadows and suddenly here was a manager who was saying how big Rangers could be.

We all knew that he was preaching to the converted, but it had been a long time since we had heard a manager saying it so powerfully and then bringing the success which would justify his claims. He made mistakes, of course, because he was still a young manager and he was now in charge of one of the biggest clubs in Britain, if not in Europe. It was obvious that there would be occasions when he would say or do something which would upset the powers that be.

The biggest mistake he made, probably, was in antagonising the Scottish Football Association, the body which rules the game in this country. He was never comfortable with their structures and they were never comfortable with what they saw as his arrogance. It was as if they were on a collision course from that fateful day when Graeme was ordered off in his debut game against Hibs at Easter Road. He didn't help himself by the stances he often took. He was not a man to back down to anyone even when it was the governing authority. They did not like to have their decisions questioned – Graeme appeared to believe that it was his job, when speaking for Rangers, to question them if he felt the club had a grievance. There were often times when the Rangers support believed that there was a vendetta against their new hero. They just could not understand how it was that Graeme Souness was in the wrong almost all of the time when there was a dispute with the people at Park Gardens. They could not accept that it was one-way traffic. When he was banned from the dug-out on one occasion he stood at the end of the tunnel – where none of the fans could see him – and he was picked up there by a television camera and when the pictures were shown the balloon went up. It was another row, another fine and another ban for Graeme and more bad blood between him and the SFA. It seemed to be a great deal of fuss over very little. The SFA could have turned a blind eye to the incident or, even if they felt they had to say something, warn him quietly rather than have the incident blown up out of all proportion. But they were not going to be budged and neither was Graeme and the inevitable happened when he left Rangers and returned south to take over as the manager of Liverpool when that job became vacant. To this day there are fans who believe that he was driven out of the Scottish game by the men in authority. They think he was persecuted.

Whether you agree with that or not there is no doubt that if the feud had continued, and there were few signs that it would ever be dampened down, then a breaking point would have been reached. Once that happened then Graeme was always going to be the loser. The SFA had the power to banish him permanently to the stand during games, refusing to allow him into the dug-out area at all. They could also have imposed ever more savage fines on him any time he stepped out of line. With Graeme's temperament he must have recognised that there were always going to be times when he would land himself in hot water with the authorities, especially as he resented the way they appeared to go after him at the slightest opportunity. Basically he did not have a great deal of time for the establishment figures in the Scottish game and so there was never any chance that peace would break out between him and the men he saw as his natural enemies.

I'm sure that he considered all of these things when the Liverpool offer came along and I'm sure, too, that he saw it as the chance for him to make a fresh start with a club he knew and in a league he was familiar with. To some extent he felt confined in the Scottish set-up, it was not big enough for him whereas the English League was. He had knocked down a lot of the parochialism in Scotland in the years he had been at Ibrox but maybe that suffocated him towards the end of his stint as the Rangers manager. Outside of Ibrox he was not liked and I always found that difficult to accept. I could understand that opposition clubs and fans would not be happy at the Rangers revival which was all down to him. Yet they should have realised that it was his enormous influence which changed the game right through the country and ALL of them benefited from the fact that Graeme Souness found the lost tribes who had vanished from the Ibrox stands and lured them back there and to every other ground in Scotland.

When Rangers went on the march again, they took an army of nearly 40,000 fans with them and provincial grounds which had not seen a sell-out situation involving Rangers in the years before his arrival certainly saw them once he had placed his imprint on the team. He put money back into the game, the whole of the game and he made other clubs ambitious. Would the changes which have taken place at Celtic have come about if Graeme Souness had not set new standards in the Scottish game? Would the crowds at the two Glasgow grounds be as big if not bigger than anything else in Britain outside of Manchester United week after week? Would you have seen the investment in top players the way there has been if Graeme Souness had not kick-started the whole thing when he walked into Ibrox in the summer of 1986? I doubt it. He was the catalyst for change. His vision for Rangers affected every other club and even now, when television and sponsorship deals are being agreed the drawing power of the Old Firm is a vital bargaining tool for the soccer establishment who disliked him so much.

Maybe he did too much, went too fast and in so doing provoked some jealousy and resentment. I can't think of any other valid reasons why he has not been lauded for dragging Scottish football into the big league as the Millennium approaches. His contribution was immense. In my opinion he carried football to a different level in Scotland. No Rangers fans ever believed that they would see Terry Butcher and Chris Woods, Ray Wilkins and Trevor Francis, Gary Stevens and Trevor Steven, Mark Hateley and Kevin Drinkell playing for their team at various times during Graeme's reign. The truth is that, initially, before the club gained its new reputation – again courtesy of Graeme – they would not have come to Scotland for any other manager. He was the man who made all of that possible because he had their respect. They looked at him after all the years at Liverpool and then his spell at Sampdoria ready and willing to play in Scotland, which they must have seen as a bit of a backwater, and they realised if Souness is going there then something big is going to happen. They were right too! Of course, there are always the snipers who point to failures in Europe and there were a few of these but Graeme was not helped when the European Union brought in the ban on the number of foreigners who could play in their tournaments. The lads he brought from England began to be phased out of the games and, as well as that, he was unlucky sometimes with the quality of opposition we came up against. It is all very well pointing to early knock-outs but I can remember two of them coming at the hands of Bayern Munich and Red Star Belgrade, scarcely the kind of teams you expect to have to face in the opening rounds. That is not an excuse, just a blunt fact of life. These are class acts.

Too many people, though, would not take that on board, happy just to snipe at us with the usual comments about being able to win in Scotland but nowhere else. It was unfair but then that's often the name of the game when people are talking or writing about Rangers and it is something we have all had to learn to live with. For Graeme, of course, it was harder to accept. He had been so used to success that even failures which would be explained away by valid reasons still hurt. The problems we found in Europe may have had something to do with his decision to quit too, though he never made his reasons public.

It seemed to be an impulsive decision, but then Graeme was always the kind of man who would act first and then think things through later so that was totally in character. But I think that there must have been times since when he regretted walking away from all he had built. He must have looked back and seen us winning that ninth successive title and wished he had been a part of all the celebrations. By then he had moved on, gone abroad, and continued to be the centre of controversy. He was as tough as nails both as a player and as a manager and he required that hardness when he was kicking off the Rangers revolution.

If he had not been able to withstand the pressure he was placed under the whole adventure might have been stillborn. He fought through it all, through the jealousies, through the rivalries and through the resentments which followed him from the very start. I was sorry when he left, saddened that he was never given the recognition he deserved for his achievements outside of the Rangers support who saw him as their messiah. He should have had better treatment and if he had he might have remained in the job. When he did walk away it was only logical that Walter Smith should be the man to take over. Certainly there were all kinds of speculation. High profile candidates were being mentioned in all the tabloids but in the dressing room we were all fairly confident that the new manager would be Walter. It made sense after all to continue along the path which he and Graeme had laid down back at the beginning. There were some amendments to be made because of the European ruling but Graeme had seen that and Walter was familiar with the new set-up which would demand more top-class Scottish players being signed by the club. A new man coming in might have upset things. Walter was privy to all the backroom thinking, having been a vital part of it for so long. When he was named as the new manager the players were delighted. Not because a single one of us thought that he would be a soft touch after Graeme, but because we had a great deal of respect for him and after the upheaval caused by Graeme's swift departure it was essential that the tremors from that should not be allowed to wreck the quest for another title.

Walter, though, was more, much more than a "safe pair of hands". He had been at Graeme's right hand from the beginning. He was Graeme's first appointment and the two of them worked well together. A lot of the time it was Walter who took the training as Graeme busied himself with other aspects of his management role. The public perception of Walter was as "Mr Nice Guy" probably because he was being compared to Graeme who did not possess that image at all. That was a bit of a misnomer as all the players knew. Walter could be as ruthless as Graeme when it was necessary. Sure he was essentially a very pleasant man but if things were not right on the field then he would make whatever hard decisions had to be made. He was every bit as demanding as Graeme and any player whose performance dropped below an expected level heard about it. Some people will be surprised to find there was another side to Walter. All I can explain is that there has to be a hard side if you are going to be a success as a football manager. If a manager shows any signs of weakness then players will take advantage of that. We have all seen it happen before but at Ibrox when Walter took over we knew it would not happen in this particular instance. Just ask Marco Negri if you don't believe me. The Italian became the equivalent for Walter of what Graham Roberts had been for Graeme – a symbol that there could only ever be one man in command of the dressing room at Ibrox. The business with Marco was a prime example of what Walter would do when he felt action was necessary for the good of the first-team squad.

There was Marco scoring goals freely during the first half of the season and then getting himself injured and after that he began to talk about leaving the club and returning to Italy, saying how unhappy he was in Scotland. All the goals he had scored could not help him one little bit because Walter would not risk having the dressing room upset by anyone saying they were not happy. Like most good managers he had a knack of being able to put his finger on anything which could cause disharmony. He had a kind of sixth sense he relied on to determine where there might be problems. The upshot was that Walter banished Marco to the reserves. There was no great fuss made by him – he just acted in the way he thought was best for the club. It did not matter how many goals he had scored for the team earlier. Nor did it matter he might have been able to score a few more on the run-in, by then Walter was relying on the club's Old Guard and unfortunately for Marco he was not seen as a part of that after talking about a return to his own country.

Walter was often under-estimated by the supporters in his time in charge. Again the failures we suffered in Europe – some of them were the result of poor performances and we have to hold our hands up to that – were held against him. Where he did not get enough praise, though, was for the magnificent run the team had in the inaugural year of the Champions League. It tends to be overlooked now but we were desperately close to winning the European Champions Cup that season. No one could question Walter's use of players and choice of tactics during that epic run we enjoyed. In the two opening rounds we won all four games, against the Danish champions Lyngby and the English champions Leeds United. It was an unforgettable run as far as the supporters and the players were concerned and the way we defeated Leeds in what was obviously billed as the Battle of Britain in the media was a special bonus for all of us. Even beating Lyngby twice was a little bit special when you consider the standard of Danish club football and our two wins, one in Copenhagen and the other at Ibrox, came only a few months after Denmark had won the European Championship in Sweden. Quite a few people had written us off because of that and because we had gone out the previous season to Sparta Prague in the opening round. We lost on away goals that time and the match had come a little too quickly for us as Walter had only commenced his re-building in the wake of Graeme's departure and in a bid to lessen the effects of the European ruling on foreign players. Big Dave McPherson had come back, while Andy Goram, David Robertson and Stuart McCall had all been signed to add to the Scottish flavour which the club now required.

Anyhow, a year further on the new players had bedded in, the team had won the League and Cup double in our first season together and we were better equipped for the challenge in Europe. In the first leg against Lyngby we won 2-0 at home with goals from Mark Hateley and Pieter Huistra and then Ian Durrant nicked the only goal of the game away from home and that set us up for the clash with Leeds. To a man the English media simply wrote us off as no-hopers, as an inferior team from an inferior league who would be far better off staying at home rather than try to topple the side they believed would go on to win the trophy that season.

Walter used all of that in his pre-match talks. Every put-down was carefully collected and then read out to us. Every sneering reference to the team and to Scottish football was passed on to us. The result was that we were all fired up when the games came along and I'm not just talking about the Scottish lads here. The Englishmen in the team were as angry as we were. They looked on the insults as being something really personal and all of them felt that they had something to prove in these two matches. One or two of them had been ignored by England, of course, including Mark Hateley, presumably because it was thought they were playing in a Mickey Mouse league. So Mark had a point to make and did he do it! The big man terrorised Leeds over the two games

49

and their defence could do nothing to stop his partnership with McCoist. In the first leg only Ally scored, with the other goal coming when their goalkeeper, John Lukic, turned a corner from Durranty into his own net. Prior to the goal from Coisty Leeds had actually had the audacity to go in front and I have never heard Ibrox as silent as it was then when Gary McAllister scored inside the opening 60 seconds of that first-leg game. Most teams would have wilted but we didn't and the comeback was very special. At Ibrox we had won 2-1 and as we repeated the scoreline down at Elland Road big Mark scored as good a goal as any he bagged in a long and successful career.

Walter's tactics were perfect and they continued that way right through the Champions League programme from which we emerged undefeated. We drew twice with Marseille who went on to win the trophy before seeing it withdrawn after allegations of bribery against them proved to be true. We were really within a fingertip of the final where Marseille beat AC Milan and having drawn with the Frenchmen twice that could have been us holding aloft the trophy. All we needed was a little bit of luck and Walter would not have had to suffer the taunts which followed him in succeeding years when we could not maintain that European drive we showed in 1992-93. It angered me when some of the fans turned on Walter and people who did not realise just how good a manager he was began to demand his resignation. It was wrong because he was a good manager. And it was wrong because he was the right manager for Rangers Football Club. Any of the players who were there with him in these glory years would tell you exactly the same as I have.

Again I was sorry when Walter decided to quit and then when the season ended so sadly it was even more heartbreaking for him and for all of us who had shared the years with him. I wish he had been able to leave clutching yet another trophy just to confirm to everyone that he was indeed the most successful manager in the history of the club. That night after the Scottish Cup Final, after we had lost to Hearts at Celtic Park, after we had failed at our last chance of winning a trophy, I don't think I have ever seen so many tears shed. All of us had known for some months that there were going to be changes but here we were with the season over and an entire era coming to a close at the same time. You really felt that Walter deserved one last trophy and I would have swapped one of the earlier Scottish Cup triumphs if I could have celebrated one last time with him and the rest of the players who were now moving on. Okay, in life you realise that nothing lasts forever, especially in football where careers are short enough and a turnover of players is now inevitable as every team chases success and managers build one team after another as they look for the trophies that the supporters demand more and more with every season that passes. This change, however, was a complete break from tradition and from the immediate past. The Chairman, David Murray, had already selected the man who was to be the new coach. Dick Advocaat who had been manager of the Dutch international team and then had been in charge of one of Holland's leading clubs, PSV Eindhoven, was set to take control in the close season. For the first time ever the club would have a non-Scot as manager.

The immediate past was jettisoned. As Walter and Archie left, they were joined out the exit door by The Goalie, Durranty, Coisty and Stuart McCall, of the Scottish brigade. Paul Gascoigne had been transferred to Middlesbrough earlier and Brian Laudrup was set to go to Chelsea under freedom of contract. The Swedish defender, Jocky Bjorklund, was also being sold while Richard Gough, who had left the year before but had returned to help the cause when injuries struck the team, was also going back to the United States. There were few survivors and I was just happy to be one of them as yet another revolution kicked in. One that was to be very different from that overseen by Mr Souness.

There was a similarity to the Souness days, however, with the spending spree Dick Advocaat embarked upon when he stepped into the position – but, as he pointed out himself, there was little option for him. He had lost half a team or more from the previous season and now he had to put together a new side almost from scratch. Not just any side either, but one which was capable of regaining the title from Celtic and, perhaps, make something of a show in the UEFA Cup.

The new man had vast experience on his side and he understood the expectations of the support from the outset. But, while he matched the millions that Graeme had spent before him he was a much more low-key personality and he admitted during that first season that he had been taken by surprise by the constant newspaper attention. In Holland he had not known that type of intensity on a daily basis and it was something he had to adapt to even while he was trying to create his OWN team and win trophies at the same time. Not very easy. Immediately he impressed all of us as a shrewd tactician and it was not long either before we realised that just like Graeme and Walter before him he could be a very hard taskmaster. As with his two predecessors everything must be done his way. If you want to stay in the first-team squad, or even stay at the club, then you have to learn to follow his instructions. A training game is stopped and the players are taken back over a move and he will keep doing that until you get it right. And if you fail once or twice then you can expect to get all kinds of hell from him. He won't let anything slip by him. That move will be repeated and repeated until you have reached the level he has demanded and only when he is satisfied will the game continue as normal. He is a fearsome perfectionist which is, I would imagine, where he has built his reputation over the years.

As far as tactics are concerned he is not a man to chop and change very often. He has a formation which he believes in. Over the years it is probably the one he has found to be the best as far as his own approach to the game is concerned. It is, if you like, a tried and trusted formula which he has come to rely upon and last season it did stand him in good stead in the various tournaments Rangers played in – especially those where the team found success! He relies on a zonal marking system and what is essentially a diamond-shaped formation and every player is given an area before taking the field and everything that happens there is your responsibility. If a goal is scored against the team and the move which has brought that goal has started in your particular zone then it's your fault and you hear about it. With both the Dutchmen on your case – the manager and his assistant, Bert van Lingen, it can be a serious matter. If you don't do the job he wants then you will be sitting out games because, essentially, he sees the modern set-up as one which requires a squad approach. He started off the season with maybe an 18-man strong first-team squad and then added to it here and there and, naturally, it is perfect for any coach to have players fighting for a place in the first team. That is the idea at any major club and it is what he is aiming for. It makes life difficult for the players but it is the only way to be successful at the top level in today's game and it is a situation all of us have to accept. No one is going to be guaranteed a first-team place. Sure, he will have players who will be his first-choice men but if they lose form, if they become a little complacent, then they will suffer in the same way as any of the other pool players.

They will be dropped and will find themselves sitting on the bench or even up in the stand. These are the harsh facts of life and when a coach is searching for success then there are few alternatives available to him in team selection. I think he took it badly with the programme of matches which have to be faced in Scotland. I don't think it is normal on the Continent to have three games a week. There are occasions when it will happen but when you are in Scotland you find that to be the norm. So it can be a little frustrating for the coaches and the players from abroad that they just cannot train every day and then gradually build towards the weekend match. Most weeks you have vital games to play on a Tuesday or a Wednesday and these take their toll on stamina and general fitness.

Most important, however, from a coaching point of view there is less time to work with the players, less time to get your ideas across, less time to become acquainted and less opportunity to concentrate on individual coaching on the days when that is felt necessary. In Scotland, and England too, the season goes from one game to another without pause and when you are with a club as big as Rangers then every game is important. There are not many chances to relax in any of the games because you are always expected to win and the opposition always, but always, raise their game against you. It is not an option for Rangers to downgrade the League Cup in importance as the Manchester United manager, Sir Alex Ferguson, has been able to do over the past few seasons. It is a trophy and our fans want to see that cup back at Ibrox even though it could well be argued that it would make sense to follow the Old Trafford example and rest players at a period of the season when you might be playing seriously vital European matches. It is a different set-up and you can see it coming as something of a culture shock to the players from other countries who have not been asked to play as many games in a season as many of them had to do last year as Rangers went to the finals of both domestic cups as well as having a lengthy run in the UEFA Cup. All of which was tremendous for the club and a magnificent start for Dick Advocaat but which took its toll on the lads over the period.

It was fortunate that the mid-season break happened for the first time in the history of our game and the lads were able to get away to Florida for a rest and for special training and, simply, to re-charge their batteries. All of them needed that. And it gave the Coach some extra weeks to work with the players on the training ground, a luxury he was not always able to enjoy back in the hothouse atmosphere of Glasgow and the constant challenges that the various tournaments threw up over the season. Of course, he has changed the routines a little. There is no day off after a midweek game now. You are still in at the ground at 11 o'clock and I could see Neil McCann taking badly to that when he first joined up from Hearts. But that is the Gaffer's way and you learn to adjust to that. Just as you learn to adapt to the different diet he put in place. Now when I went to Ibrox at first I found it a change from St Mirren, as well as being a world away from Clyde, because Graeme Souness had brought back from Italy where he had played with Sampdoria the habit of eating pasta after training. He had lunches organised at the Stadium and we would go upstairs and eat together. But we were also allowed a bit of latitude and so we could also get bacon rolls or egg rolls or sausage rolls from the kitchen. That stopped last season because Dick Advocaat brought his own dietary beliefs with him. No more bacon butties! Now we were encouraged to eat chicken with rice or salmon with rice and that type of main dish as well as pasta. But it's always rice you have – no chips and the meat or fish is grilled and everything is done very well. We have weight checks every month but that is not new. We always did have that. But it shows that the game has changed dramatically from the old days, or even when I first became a senior. Every country has a different look at diet but the essentials are the same and the usual eating habits of Scots players are no longer seen as the ideal. You do feel the benefit though and that is the object of the whole exercise, remember.

It has been interesting to see how the club has affected the coaches and the new players. Sure they knew that they were joining a major club, otherwise they would not have come to Ibrox in the first place. But over the season you could see the realisation dawn on them just how massive Rangers can be. When they saw the support week after week and when they saw how many people travelled abroad to watch the European ties and then when we went to Florida in January they saw the hundreds of exiled fans who wanted to watch them train and see them play and generally make them all welcome. I have seen the passion that the support have always shown for the club rub off on the foreign players and I have seen the fans adopt heroes from Russia and Holland, from Italy and Germany, from Finland and France, from Argentina and Australia, from England and Chile. There are no barriers now and while our fathers would never have expected to see such an invasion from other countries the supporters of today have accepted everyone. These have been very exciting times for the club but, always, there has been talk of youth development.

The Chairman, David Murray, and the Coach, Dick Advocaat have been planning a new training ground and they seem determined that there will be a soccer academy there which will unearth young Scottish talent and help the players of the future hone their skills. It has to be stressed that as well as bringing in players from Europe the Coach has also brought in Scottish players such as Colin Hendry and Neil McCann and has stated that he would like to buy more. If the youth programme can be set up then that would ensure that in the years to come there will always be Scottish players at Ibrox and while the stars from abroad have all made powerful contributions Rangers are a Scottish club and will always remain that. I am one of those people who believe that the talent is still out there and we have seen young Barry Ferguson blossom in the past year. There are more talented players where he came from and once the training ground has been constructed and the academy is up and running Rangers will be able to get the very best of the youngsters in Scotland. The players, meanwhile, will benefit from state-of-the-art facilities which will encourage them to work harder at the game and help them to make it as professionals. The future of the club could lie there rather than in buying new players every summer. Nowadays you must always buy but it would be terrific if Rangers could get to the same stage as Manchester United who still spend huge sums of money in the transfer market and yet are still able to find and develop their own players and to push them into the first team. They have the balance right and that is what every club must take as an example.

Whether you will have players and coaches staying with one club as long as I have done and as long as Walter Smith did is another matter. I would like to think that my young namesake will maybe last the course as long as I have. In the main, though, players will move on from club to club as a result of the Bosman ruling and I tend to think that coaches will do the same. That trend is there for everyone to see on the Continent and it seems likely to spread to Britain in due course.

But no matter what trends affect the coaches and the players of today or in the future there is one thing I am convinced of and that is that Rangers Football Club will always create its own special magic. Players may come and go but Rangers will remain.

5

CHAPTER FIVE

A Brush With The Tartan Army

It's always been a matter of some regret to me that I have only managed to win nine caps for my country in an international career which began 10 years ago but seemed to be constantly interrupted by injuries. To be honest I have had more call-offs than I have had caps. I always knew that Craig Brown believed in my ability. He had me at Clyde when I broke through into the senior game and then he picked me for the Under-21 team when I was still with St Mirren. I received my first full cap while Andy Roxburgh was the international team manager and I always had a feeling at the back of my mind that Craig's influence had helped to carry me into the squad.

I had only been around half a season with Rangers when I was picked for the first time. That was when we were trying to qualify for the 1990 World Cup Finals and a match had been arranged against the host nation, Italy, in Perugia. It was only a friendly but it was a glamour game and a crucial one for the team as we were trying to qualify for these Finals from a group which included France, Yugoslavia, Norway and Cyprus – a very, very formidable group from which to qualify. I was fortunate enough to be part of two important victories which helped Scotland get to Italy, I came on as a substitute in Cyprus when Richard Gough scored an amazing injury-time winner in a match which seemed to go on forever. And I was on from the start in the match against France which we won 2-0 at Hampden..

For various reasons – mostly to do with my illness, which I dealt with in another chapter, and my injuries – I didn't get back into the international squad for four years and even then it was for three relatively unimportant matches, twice against Malta, one of them only as a substitute; and then against Estonia at home. The team won all three, it would have been a major shock if we had not done so, but the results did not get Scotland to the World Cup Finals in the United States the following summer. Switzerland went instead. Andy Roxburgh then quit the job to take up his post with UEFA and Craig took over, which could have been a signal perhaps for yours truly to make a permanent niche on the Scotland scene. I did play in two friendly games, when we beat Austria in Vienna 2-1 and I appeared as a substitute and then we were defeated by Holland in Utrecht by the same margin and I was again pulled on from the bench. That was on the eve of the Dutch departure for the World Cup Finals in the States and, funnily enough, Dick Advocaat was the man in charge of their team back then. There was a lot of controversy that night and the Gaffer was at the centre of it when Ruud Gullit, who had agreed to return to the national side, walked off at half-time and didn't return, then announced that he would not go the States apparently because there had been a disagreement between him and the man who was to become the Rangers' manager four years further down the line. That maybe underlines to you the strength of character that the Gaffer possesses and that ruthless streak that every top manager I have known has had.

It's possible that after that comeback Craig Brown might have persevered with me but that was the time my various back problems struck me down and I was missing games for Rangers and suffering quite badly and so the opportunity, which I am sure would have been there, disappeared yet again.

It returned just briefly and on this occasion, the last time I played in fact, it all ended in tears after I was involved in a major row with the Scotland supporters who had travelled to Monaco in force for the World Cup qualifying game against Estonia. The game had been re-scheduled for that rather exotic venue after the floodlighting problems in Tallinn had seen the Estonians fail to turn up in time even though the FIFA official in charge had warned them that they must start the match at an earlier hour because their temporary lights were not up to the standard required for a top-level fixture. Initially it looked as if Scotland would be awarded a victory in the match, as laid down in the rules which govern World Cup games, and that would have given us three points as well as a three-goal boost in the battle for qualification where we were going head to head against Austria. Then that was all changed and the Estonians were given the opportunity of staging their home game at a neutral venue. Monaco was the designated spot and that's where we went. It is a journey that I now wish I had never made. At the time I was named as a member of the squad I was excited at the thought of getting back on the international scene, knowing of course that the World Cup Finals were looming not too far ahead and that a win over the Estonians could just about carry us there. It handed me a bit of a lift – and then came the sad and sorry ending and I have never been given the opportunity to play again, mainly I have to say because of my injury problems.

Anyhow, we did not get the result we wanted that day in Monaco. And a 0-0 draw was not the result those travelling supporters had been expecting, either. When we came off the field they were booing the players and I was one of the targets for their anger. I was walking off alongside Colin Calderwood and the fans were leaning over from the stands giving us all kinds of abuse. Big Colin was applauding them. Now I know that not all of the fans were booing but I turned to him and said "Don't clap them" and I meant it because of the way many had been behaving. And in the frustration of the moment I did swear. Anyhow, it was just my luck that there was a television mike near us as we got to the touchline and it picked up my comment and the words were broadcast back home. When we returned the outcry was unbelievable. It was as if I committed murder. The whole affair was blown out of all proportion and I found myself in the middle of this controversy which was the very last thing I needed having just returned to the squad after being absent for three years.

All of this happened simply because I reacted to the supporters who were yelling abuse at the players. I mean, we were just as disappointed and upset as the fans were that day. We knew that we had slipped up, we knew that we had to live with the fact that we had blown a chance of just about clinching qualification for the World Cup Finals in France. And I did not see there was the slightest reason to applaud people who were slagging us off. Things were not improved by the agent I had at that time who issued a statement saying that I was speaking about the Estonian players and not the supporters and that simply aggravated the situation. Okay, he was trying to protect me, trying to cover up because he thought that was his job. Of course, it backfired totally and I was caught between a feeling of loyalty for the agent and the need to tell the truth no matter what the consequences were going to be. The one way out that I saw was to speak to Craig Brown and I did that. However, all I said then was that I was ready to apologise to the people who were sitting in their living rooms back home watching television and who heard me swear. There was no way that I was ever going to apologise to the supporters who had been jeering us so viciously from the stands in Monaco. I also felt aggrieved that I should be a target for so much of the abuse when I had been on the field for just 20 minutes as a substitute and I think that was a sign that the Tartan Army does not contain as many Rangers supporters as it once did. In the days of the Home International Championships apparently the bulk of the Scotland support came from Rangers but all that has altered over the years. I think that has something to do with the way Graeme Souness was treated by the SFA and then, after that, the Duncan Ferguson court case did not improve relationships between our club and its supporters and the authorities.

I'm certain that the attitude of the football bosses over the two of them saw a huge portion of the Rangers fans turn against the SFA and, in turn, give up supporting the national side. Mostly the Tartan Army, these self-styled "best fans in the world" come mainly from areas outside Glasgow and are supporters of other Scottish teams rather than Rangers. So I suppose that being an Ibrox player was another reason for me to get it in the neck but I was not prepared to take it. They were wrong and yet they wanted it to appear that I was the one who was out of order and I was not willing to take on that role. Not for anyone and especially not for people who were jeering a team who still had the chance to qualify for France and which eventually did get there as the best-placed second team from all the European qualifying groups. It was a remarkable achievement when you consider that Sweden were also in the section and they had finished in third place in the previous

Finals in the United States. None of that mattered to the Tartan Army foot soldiers who hurled their venom at us as we trudged off the field in Monaco.

It was suggested back then that it was a one-off. I was never convinced of that and last season the country's captain, Gary McAllister, was driven out of the national side by the same kind of disgraceful booing that we had been forced to listen to a couple of years earlier. If there was ever a player who did not deserve to have that happen to him, it was Gary. He had captained the team through two successful qualifying campaigns, to reach Euro 96 in England and then to get to France. Then, after playing in the games which saw us qualify for France he was injured, needed an operation and was not fit enough to play in the Finals. It was a real blow for him and here he was coming back, after being successful with his club following injury, and playing against the Czech Republic at Celtic Park and when the team lost 2-1, being jeered so savagely that Craig Brown took him off the field early to protect him from the mindless morons who were making it clear that they did not want him there. It was terrible and I felt for Gary as I recalled what had happened in Monaco and realised that there are times when the Tartan Army for all their high profile good behaviour can act as badly as any other fans.

On that occasion they behaved shamefully. What had Gary McAllister done to deserve all of that? There were suggestions that he had never been forgiven for missing a penalty against England at Wembley during Euro 96. No mention, of course, that he did score a vital penalty against Belarus en route to France. Nor any mention of the way he had always been ready to play for his country and had never, ever shirked responsibility on the field. I thought the whole thing was scandalous and when you also read that he had received hate mail from these supposed fans it made you wonder if it was all worth it. After a few days to think things over Gary decided that it was not. I have to say that I agreed totally with him. He has had a difficult enough job piecing his career together again after that very serious injury and trying to steer his club, Coventry, clear of the threat of relegation from the Premiership. He did not need to be called to his country's colours again only to find himself the butt of abuse from people who are not intelligent enough to look at that player's career and see what he has achieved and what he did for his country.

Gary played 57 times for Scotland and, sure, he might have had the odd bad game but he was a player who was always respected by his fellow professionals. You only have to look at the success he had at Leeds and even now how, as a veteran, he is a key player for Coventry. But he had had enough and the Tartan Army rank and file who drove him out of the national team should feel ashamed of themselves. It did more than just affect Gary McAllister, it hurt members of his family who were in the stand that night and who heard the venom directed at him by these so-called supporters.

After Monaco and my own little problem – and it was small compared to Gary's troubles – I said that I would be ready to play again if Craig selected me. Craig said nothing that had happened would stop me being picked by him if he thought it appropriate. It has never happened. I have had more than my share of injuries and that has meant that I have not been available when any of the squads have been named. Now, after the Gary McAllister incident, I don't know what I would do. It is not in my nature to walk away from any problem so I would probably play again if I was chosen, though I don't see that happening again. My Scotland career stalled after just nine full caps. I wish there could have been more. I envied the other players when they went off to play in the World Cup or European Finals because these are the tournaments every player dreams about being part of. But it was not to be. Injuries and illness which blighted a great portion of my Rangers career intervened too often to allow me a real run with the international team.

Oh, and just to nail the rumours which used to rage when players at Ibrox called off from Scotland fixtures, I have to say that while Graeme Souness would have preferred the lads not to go on international duty when the club was at a particularly crucial stage of the season, he never actually stopped anyone from reporting. He would give you a few verbals but nothing more than that. It was always left to each individual player to decide whether or not he should go with Scotland. In my experience when players were fit they joined up with the squad and if they were unfit to play they stayed back at Ibrox for treatment. Poor Graeme had had enough stick without being blamed for that!

6

CHAPTER SIX

The First Five Years ...

I joined Rangers because it was the club I had always followed and the club I had always wanted to play for but I also wanted success from the game and that was always more likely to come if I was at Ibrox. Almost every player who signs for the club will tell you that they want to win medals – and almost every one of them does so – and I was no exception. Which was why the first few months after I signed were frustrating for me. I only played for eight games after signing and I watched from the sidelines as the club lost to Dunfermline in the Scottish Cup and followed that by losing to Steaua Bucharest, the Romanian champions, in the European Cup quarter-finals. While I had signed before these games I was not eligible for any of them which made it all the harder for me to accept the results, knowing I was powerless to help the team. It was disappointing from another aspect too because a few months earlier I had been collecting my first medal with St Mirren after we had won the Scottish Cup against Dundee United. That had been a good tournament for me. I scored goals in the quarter-final against Morton, in the semi-final against Hearts and then scored the only goal of the game at Hampden against the Tannadice team. That result also meant that I was arriving at Rangers as a winner so it was all the more galling that, while the team had won the League Cup before I arrived, they lost the Scottish Cup and the title after I had signed.

Looking back down the years I find myself taking more satisfaction from the Scottish Cup Final now than I did at the time. I was just a youngster, remember, 20 years old, and while I scored and St Mirren took the trophy, I was really upset at my own performance. The goal apart, I felt that I had not made a genuine contribution to the victory. Now, of course, older and maybe a little bit wiser, I realise that when people look at the record books all they will see is the scoreline and the fact that I scored the Cup-winning goal. They won't have a clue as to how I performed in the game itself. Yet it was the poorest Cup display I gave that season. I know that myself.

The strike, however, remains among my top five goal scoring memories. I can recall getting away from the United defender, John Clark, who was a big, strong player and then I shot and the ball flew into the net. That brought me my first medal and it gave St Mirren their first Scottish Cup success in thirty years. You know, winning a trophy with one of the smaller clubs is a little bit special because no one ever expects it to happen. All along we were told by the supporters that we would not make the Final, that St Mirren teams always went so far and then things went horribly wrong. That year the predictions from Paisley were that we would lose out in the semi-final and all the hopes and dreams would be stored away for another year just as had happened so often in the past. So when we went past Hearts it was something of a milestone, a kind of a landmark for the players I suppose, although we realised that Dundee United would be formidable opponents. That was the season that their manager, Jim McLean, guided them to the Final of the UEFA Cup, defeating the likes of Barcelona and Borussia Mönchengladbach on the way to the two-legged showdown with IFK Gothenburg. They were a class team and we knew that and to this day I believe that we caught them at exactly the right time. They had the second leg of the UEFA Cup Final at Tannadice four days after the Scottish Cup Final. They had played in more than 70 matches that season as they moved into the Hampden game against us and, to be honest, I think they were utterly exhausted. All the games, so many of them major ones, too, had taken their toll and we benefited from that.

Of course, we were a good side as well, difficult to beat because our manager, Alex Smith, had all of us working for each other. We all wired in when we were in trouble during a match and no one ever let one of his team-mates down. The manager had instilled a great spirit in the dressing room and the Cup run – and eventual success – stemmed from that. I saw the same thing in later years at

Ibrox and nothing can beat a team which has happy players in the dressing room who are always ready to help each other out on the field. That is a recipe for success and I saw it for the first time at Love Street. I wasn't there long but I enjoyed my time with Saints and I would never say a bad word about the club. They handed me my Premier League apprenticeship.

They gave me my first opportunity to win a medal. And playing with them allowed me the chance to impress Graeme Souness and fulfil my life's ambition to play for Rangers. When you're younger you don't always realise the full implication of what is going on round about you. In the last couple of years it has struck me just how important that period of my career was to my future development as a player. Also, I have realised how precious that Cup win was to the town of Paisley, to the loyal supporters as well as to the players and Alex Smith. There is a point of view now which suggests that the smaller clubs such as St Mirren will never be able to win the major trophies again because of the direction the game has taken. I would not like to think that. I would dearly love to see St Mirren fighting their way back into the Premier League and making a go of things when they get there. I will always have a soft spot for them and I hope they do well. When I left it was because I had to make the break but the money they received for me and the Cup Final goal must have helped pay the club back for the start they handed me in the top level of the game in Scotland.

Anyhow, after leaving in February 1988 it was on to Rangers and coming to terms with the fact that the Souness revolution had stalled in Graeme's second season in charge. When he took over and won the Premier League in his first season it was generally believed among Rangers supporters that he would just go on and on winning. That season the club took the League Cup only while Celtic won the Championship and the Scottish Cup but, being inside Ibrox, I knew the feelings around the club and the ambitions and when I signed, Graeme had told me the level he intended to carry the club towards. So, while there might have been some misgivings among the support, I had no qualms at all about Rangers' future. From that first meeting with Graeme when the deal was being completed I knew deep down that the winners' medals would be arriving on a regular basis, season after season, although I have to say that I never thought there would be quite as many of them! But Graeme had told me that he wanted to take Rangers onto greater and greater success and he gave me an idea of the quality of players he was going to be bringing in and exactly how he wanted the team to play the game.

He talked with such conviction in the manager's office that day that I realised then it was all going to work for him. Listening to him talk it was also clear to me that I was now moving to a different level in the game and I don't mean any disrespect to St Mirren when I say that. It had been a step up going from Clyde to Love Street – but this was a giant leap upwards and it goes without saying that I have never regretted listening to Graeme Souness and believing the promises he made to me that day. All of them have come true and my only little regret is that Graeme was not there to enjoy the successes which arrived after he had returned to Liverpool for his spell as manager.

The following year was my first full season as a Rangers player and just as Graeme had forecast, the medals started to flow …

There was a victory over Aberdeen in the League Cup Final, a marvellous game which we won 3-2 and I scored one of the goals. Really, that strike owed a lot to the experience and strength of Kevin Drinkell who was playing up front for us that day. Drinks was not always given the credit he was due in his time with Rangers. He was a marvellous professional and he showed all he had learned in the game in that moment which allowed me to snatch the goal. If you look back at the video of that Final you can see Kevin just taking big Alex McLeish out of things when the ball comes over. That little move, using all of his strength, gave me the space I needed to try a shot when the ball broke to me. I caught it just right and I knew when I struck it that it was going to go in. That was the first of all the medals I have won with Rangers and the Championship medal – another first for me – was to arrive at the end of that debut season.

That was memorable enough but two of our results against Celtic that year – who remember had won the League and Cup double the previous season – were unforgettable as far as I am concerned. We won the first Old Firm game of the season at Ibrox

JUST ONE OF US... Fergie enjoys spending time with fellow Rangers supporters, here he signs autographs after winning nine-in-a-row at Tannadice

FIRM FRIENDS… Ian Ferguson and Peter Grant had their fair share of midfield battles during Old Firm clashes – with Fergie usually coming out on top

TRAIN OF THOUGHT… even in training Ferguson still gives his all

*HAT'S A BEAUTY… goal hero Ian celebrates St Mirren's 1-0 Scottish Cup Final
victory over Dundee United in 1987 – the first trophy of his career*

TURNING THE OTHER CHEEK… Fergie walks away from Celtic forward Paolo di Canio at the end of Rangers' crucial 1-0 victory at Parkhead in 1997

CUP A LOAD OF THAT... As usual Fergie is in the middle of the celebrations as Rangers complete the domestic treble at Hampden with a 1-0 win over Celtic

IBROX CHEER... it's pure joy for Fergie as he celebrates Erik Bo Andersen's strike against Celtic in the 1997 New Year game at Ibrox which Gers won 3-1

LOOKING DISHY! Fergie and his Ibrox team-mates get ready to tuck in at the midfielder's testimonial dinner at the Thistle Hotel in 1998

BLOOD, SWEAT AND CHEERS… Ferguson always gives his all in the Light Blue jersey, and that involves taking a few knocks along the way

PUTTING THEM IN THE SHADE… Fergie is now the longest serving player at Ibrox

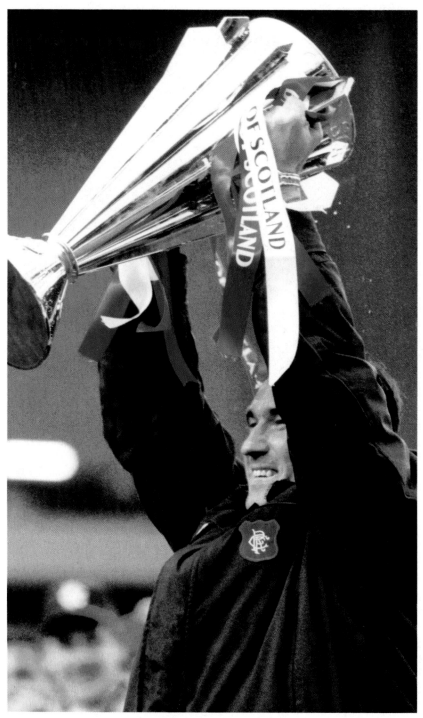

FEELING CHAMPION… As one of the few Scots left at Ibrox, Ferguson proudly lifts the Scottish Premier League trophy above his head at the end of the 1998/99 season

*FIVE ALIVE… Fergie joins Richard Gough in congratulating goal heroes Gordon
Durie and Brian Laudrup after Gers' 5-1 Scottish Cup Final win over Hearts in 1996*

SHOOTING STAR… Fergie was a key player for the Blues during their Champions League run of 1992/93 – here finding the back of the net against CSKA Moscow

HAUL OF FAME… Ferguson shows off his amazing haul of medals. In 12 years at Ibrox he has collected 18 winners' and four runners-up medals

BORN LEADERS… Richard Gough and Ian Ferguson formed the backbone of the nine-in-a-row side for Rangers, both winning the ball in vital areas and inspiring others

LOOKING BACK… Fergie can reminisce with a smile about his career at Ibrox

*PERFECT MATCH… Ian and wife Suzanne on their wedding day, and the happy couple
have since added two kids to the family, Stephanie and Jordan*

FLAG DAY… With another trophy in the bag Fergie can afford to have a seat and take in the atmosphere as the Gers celebrate six-in-a-row

STAR IN STRIPES… Even out of the blue Fergie was a star for Rangers

BOARD GAMES… Despite a broken leg ruling Ally McCoist out of Gers' title celebrations at Broomfield in 1993, Fergie made sure Coisty was part of the fun

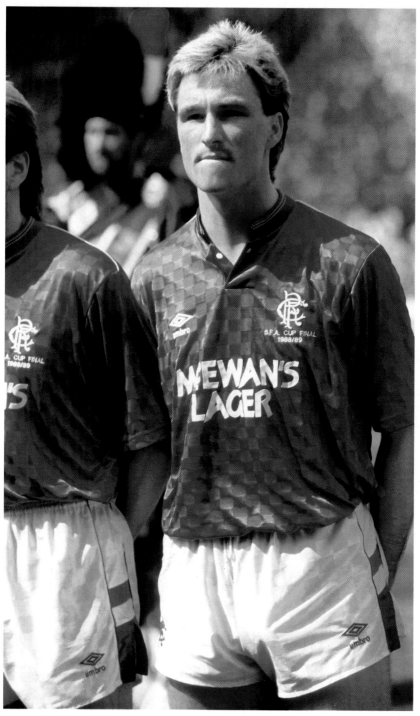

PROUD AS PUNCH… Fergie lines up for Rangers before a Cup Final

BALL BOY… Ian Ferguson's contribution to the Rangers midfield is not just limited to tough tackling, he is also capable of playing some exquisite passes to split a defence

LET ME SHOW YOU AROUND... Ian Ferguson looks at home in Rangers'
magnificent trophy room

DRIVING FORCE... Ian's strong running and stunning strikes from the
edge of the box became an early feature of his play under Souness at Ibrox

GRIN AND BEAR IT… Despite Dick Advocaat's clear out of the Ibrox old guard, Fergie has remained a valuable part of the Rangers first-team squad

MAKE MINE A TREBLE... Fergie celebrates the first part of Gers' glorious treble of 1998/99, a 2-1 League Cup Final win over St Johnstone at Parkhead

CROWD PLEASER... When Fergie is injured he likes nothing better than joining the supporters in the stands to cheer on the boys in blue

SMILES BETTER… Fergie celebrates back at Ibrox after the 1999 Scottish Cup Final

BLUE GRIT… Few players have shown more passion in a Rangers jersey than Fergie

TWO OF A KIND… True blues Ian Ferguson and John Brown have become the best of friends during their time together at Ibrox

HEAD FOR HEIGHTS… It was Fergie's wonderful performances for St Mirren in their victorious Scottish Cup run of 1987 that caught the eye of Graeme Souness

POWERING ON… As he enters his twelfth season with the Ibrox club Fergie is still going strong and could play a big part in the busy year ahead for the club

5-1 and followed that by winning 4-1 when Celtic returned to the Stadium for the traditional New Year fixture. Glorious victories both of them but the first one is still tinged with regret for me because I felt that we could have gone on and scored seven goals and gained revenge for the League Cup Final defeat of 1958 when Celtic defeated Rangers by that margin. It was certainly possible.

I don't mean this in a bad way, but Graeme Souness came on as a substitute after we had scored the fifth goal. Now we had more than 20 minutes left to play and by this time they were, as you would expect, demoralised. There was ample time to get another two goals and that was what was in my thoughts and then when Graeme appeared the pattern of the game altered dramatically. I just don't think it had registered with him that Rangers had once lost 7-1 to Celtic and that here was the chance for revenge. He was only thinking that the game was won, that five goals was a serious "doing" and that all we had to do now was play the ball about, keep possession and, to some extent, take the mickey out of the Celtic players by not allowing them a touch of the ball. That was what he wanted to do and he imposed himself on the game in that second half with that in mind. Meanwhile, myself and Coisty and Durranty were all looking at each other and saying "What's he doing here, what's he up to?" and, of course, Graeme was not looking at the situation as we were. I enjoyed the win but I will always see that game as a missed opportunity. I truly believe that we could have scored seven that day. The game was in our grasp and we had enough time to get the two goals which would have been so important to our support. Graeme just didn't understand what was at stake regarding the history of the Old Firm. He wanted the points, he wanted to savour the victory, but he wanted to do it in his own way and, while that worked out all right, it was one of the few occasions I thought he made a mistake as manager because it was a chance to make our own little bit of history and the fans would have loved that.

They loved it anyway as they celebrated the goals from Ally McCoist, who scored twice, Ray Wilkins, Kevin Drinkell and Mark Walters. And they loved it all over again when we won 4-1 at New Year even though we had lost 3-1 to Celtic at Parkhead between times. This time the goals came from Mark Walters, one of these a penalty, Terry Butcher, and myself. It was my first Old Firm goal and later that term it seemed I had scored my second in a 2-1 win in the last game against Celtic that season but Coisty claimed it. He was chasing some goal-scoring record or other, which was no surprise, and he was involved close in when the ball crossed the line.

He said he had bundled it into the net and it was his goal – which, again, was no surprise – and I didn't argue. It was enough for me that the goal had counted and that it had given us our third win over Celtic that season. To be fair, I don't know who got the final touch. What had happened was that we had been awarded a free-kick some 30 yards from goal after Coisty had been fouled by Peter Grant who had been snapping at his heels – no surprise there either! Ray Wilkins touched the ball to me and I shot and I still remember to this day that as I struck through the ball I knew that I had connected really well with it. Pat Bonner reached it but because of the force of the ball it spun away from him and up in the air and back towards the goal line. He was on the ground by now trying to scramble back and then Coisty and Chris Morris rushed in and the three of them were there and the ball was in the net and Coisty was celebrating. I didn't mind one little bit because the goal meant we had won the game and the result was important because it came in a glorious streak of form which saw us go 12 games undefeated to clinch the Championship and, as part of that run, we also won nine games on the trot. It was a tremendous finish to the season and even though we missed out on a treble when Celtic beat us in the Scottish Cup Final it could not kill the feeling I had inside me that we were heading for great times ahead. The Hampden defeat by Celtic – and there was doubt about the goal they scored – was the only serious blemish on the season. We had gone into the game with injuries and Graeme, who had been phasing himself out that season, was even forced to pick himself even though he had made only a handful of appearances, mainly coming on from the substitutes' bench. It was another sign of the Cup jinx he had suffered when he was a player at Liverpool and which had seemed to dog his footsteps when he decided to take over as player-manager of Rangers. He took the defeat badly, not that he was ever very good at accepting a loss, because he knew that the treble should have been completed and would have been completed if things had only gone our way both before and during that game. But as I was only at the beginning of my Rangers career I was able to overcome the disappointment of the Final and savour the two winners' medals I had won just as Graeme Souness had promised me I would.

The next season brought a significant breakthrough for the club before a ball had been kicked. Never one to back away from controversy Graeme nicked in ahead of Celtic and signed Maurice Johnston from the French First Division club Nantes where the Scottish international striker had spent two years after leaving Parkhead. Quite apart from being the club's first high-profile Catholic player Mo had been involved in a signing tug-of-war between Rangers and Celtic. Our Old Firm rivals had paraded him as a major new signing but all of the necessary paperwork had not been completed and so Graeme made his move and was successful and Celtic were left with a great deal of egg on their faces while Rangers had signed a prolific goal scorer. That added to the problems that Mo was always going to face. Not only was he a Catholic playing for Rangers he had also, as far as the Celtic fans were concerned, turned his back on them and reneged on a signing deal. To be honest, I don't know how he handled it all. How he got through all of it while still playing superbly and scoring goals week in and week out remains a mystery to me. He even had to come into the Stadium with a bodyguard because of the threats which were hurled in his direction. No one at Rangers dared ignore them and so there we had Mo and the bodyguard every day at training.

He soon settled in and some of the credit for breaking the ice with him has to go to our kit man, Jimmy Bell, who is a Rangers supporter through and through. Jimmy was not best pleased at the development, initially, and he was giving Walter Smith stick at our Italian training camp, Il Ciocco, where we were based when the signing was completed. Anyhow, the following day when Mo arrived Jimmy set up a table for one in the dining room and we all thought that he was going to sit there himself to register his protest. But that wasn't it at all. Instead it was a seat on his own for Mo who immediately saw the wind-up and accepted the kidding and from then on everything was fine. It had been a very difficult situation for him and Jimmy had helped him laugh his way through it. Inside the club everything was fine. Outside the club Mo was under massive pressure and I don't know how he did not crack. I can tell you, I would not have been able to do what he did. All the money in the world would not have tempted me into the position he was put in.

It was incredible that he was able to score the goals he did score and play the way he did play and I would never allow anyone to say a bad word about Maurice Johnston because he never gave less than 100 per cent in any game he played for Rangers. He became a huge asset because he was an exceptional front player and a fantastic finisher. He scored 15 League goals for us that season as we took the title again with Aberdeen second and Hearts third. Unfortunately it was the only trophy we did win. We lost to Aberdeen in the League Cup Final when Paul Mason scored twice for them while we had to be content with a Mark Walters' penalty and we slipped out of the Scottish Cup when we lost to Celtic away from home in an early round of the tournament.

The League, naturally, was the major priority and we did win that with a seven-point margin from the two chasing teams from Pittodrie and Tynecastle. Mo scored the only goal of the game in his Ibrox Old Firm debut after we had drawn earlier at Parkhead. Then in the New Year game a Nigel Spackman strike gave us our win while Mo saved himself for getting another goal at Ibrox when we beat Celtic 3-0 – the other goals were from penalty kicks taken by Mark Walters and Ally McCoist – in the last Old Firm match of that season. As well as his contributions against Celtic he scored the only goal of the game against Aberdeen at Ibrox and then did the same against Hearts in the first quarter of the season, so you can see how vital a player he was. That was my second Championship and if it is remembered as Mo Johnston's year then I, for one, would not argue with that tag. He deserves any kind of accolade for going through what he went through and still being the ultimate professional every time he walked on to the pitch. He was incredible that season and there was more to come from him as we should all have realised. Graeme was never going to sit back and be content with the playing resources he had. He was always looking to improve things and to do that he decided that a different frontline partnership was required at Ibrox for the next season and so he went out and persuaded Mark Hateley to give up the sunshine and the luxury of Monaco where he had been playing in the French First Division in exchange for the glamours of Govan. Even Graeme's remarkable powers of persuasion must have been tested when they first met to discuss the deal but he did it.

Somehow or other he was successful in convincing Mark to give up the Mediterranean lifestyle to which he had become accustomed and, instead, choose to play for Rangers. It was a move which excited controversy among our own supporters because Graeme now had three top-class front men, McCoist, Johnston and Hateley and despite the goals which Coisty had scored so regularly it was the partnership of Johnston and Hateley which the manager preferred. The fans' hero, Ally, was often left sitting out the action on the bench, though in that season the three of them combined to score 34 League goals between them.

It was a momentous season that one. We won the League Cup again and it was a tournament which was kind to us over the years – in stark contrast to the cruel results we found almost inevitably in the Scottish Cup. We beat Celtic in the Hampden Final with goals from Mark Walters and Richard Gough but they claimed revenge when they knocked us out of our jinx tournament in the quarter-final. Then, near the end of the season, Graeme received the call from Anfield and after much soul-searching went south to take over at the club he had served so successfully as a player. Walter Smith was named the new manager which was the only choice the Chairman, David Murray, could have made. Walter had worked so closely with Graeme since the start and he knew the players and the club and he knew the long-term strategies which had been worked out so carefully to ensure that Rangers stayed at the very top.

The immediate worry, however, was just how we were going to do that because injuries had decimated the player pool and we were limping towards the finishing line with Aberdeen, our closest challengers, looking stronger and stronger in each succeeding week. That season had seen the start of my illness worries and I came into the side only towards that troubled end to the campaign when Walter was being forced to play makeshift line-ups as he bid to keep the championship run going. We lost 3-0 to Celtic away from home, I remember, but then we put things together and had three wins in succession, against St Johnstone at Ibrox, St Mirren at Love Street when young Sandy Robertson scored the only goal of the game and then against Dundee United at home when I was the sole scorer. By then it seemed that we would hang on in there with just two games to go and the last one being at home.

That was when Aberdeen were the visitors in a game which could still decide the title even after the three solid results we had registered. Then, just as it appeared that we had fought our way through the worst of the slump, we went to Motherwell and we lost 3-0 in one of the worst performances I can remember the team giving when the chips were down. It was a terrible result and now the pressure was being heaped on us as the last game loomed with Aberdeen now knowing that a draw would be enough to give them the Championship when they travelled down to Glasgow to meet us. They were now in the driving seat. They could dictate the way the game would be played because they did have two alternative routes to the title – either with a win or a draw. We did not have that luxury.

I think we had something like half a team missing because of injury as well as players being strapped up just to try to get them through the 90 minutes. In fact, John Brown took a pain-killing jag in a bid to help the club to the title. Yet, in spite of all that, I had a feeling that this was a game we were going to win. I don't know to this day what made me feel so confident, whether it was the atmosphere around the Stadium when I arrived for the game, whether it was the way the fans were reacting when they saw the players or whether it was just one of these hunches we get at one time or another. It was unusual for me to feel that way. My nature is such that I'm normally looking at the downside but not that day. I can remember sitting upstairs having a bite to eat with Coisty and saying to him "We're going to win today, we're really going to do it" and totally believing it myself because the whole atmosphere just felt right. Yet it looked as if I was going to be wrong when the game kicked off and they had two early chances to score. Their two Dutchmen, Peter Van De Ven and Hans

Gillhaus, both had scoring opportunities. Van De Ven tried to chip Chris Woods first of all but only succeeded in playing the ball into the keeper's hands. Then Gillhaus had an opening which he squandered and I was beginning to doubt my own feelings. To add to all the pre-match worries Tom Cowan was stretchered off with a broken leg, John Brown broke down and had to limp out of the action and Mark Walters pulled his hamstring. But Mark Hateley was the hero of heroes that afternoon. He scored twice and his goals gave us the win and the Championship.

It was a strange looking side which took a ragged lap of honour, though. I think I was the only outfield player who ended the game in the same position I had had at kick-off. Terry Hurlock ended up playing at left-back, Mark Hateley completed the game as our centre-half, Mo Johnston was beside me in midfield with Coisty having come off the bench and gone up front on his own and yet we had done it. There were a lot of winners in that team, even the depleted team which Walter was forced to field, and the even more depleted team which finished the 90 minutes. That day was memorable for all of us because we had been able to win against all the odds. Yet even as I celebrated I felt sympathy for my old St Mirren gaffer, Alex Smith, who was manager of Aberdeen. He must have arrived at Ibrox believing that his team would be champions, that his players would be taking the trophy north to Pittodrie later that day and then it was snatched away from them. The Championship was there within their grasp and we ended up the winners. At the start they must have thought they would win comfortably but whenever Mark struck with the opening goal it was all over. Nothing was going to stop us after that and as a finale to the season it was one of the best in all the 10 successes I have known in my years with Rangers, nothing since then has topped the feelings I had when that final whistle blew. Excitement. Relief. Immense satisfaction. And a real pride in the way the players and Walter had been able to handle the very dangerous situation we had found ourselves in as the season dragged towards its end.

That game signalled the end of another era at Ibrox because now Walter was in charge, he was his own man and he had changes to make, with some of them being forced upon him by the alterations to the rules governing European competition. Only three foreign players were to be allowed and the foreign tag applied to English players as well as those from abroad, so there were decisions for Walter to make and he knew that he had to bring in more Scottish players as a matter of necessity if we were to be able to play in Europe without constantly chopping and changing the team from the 11 who were able to play in the domestic tournaments to one which was allowed by the European Union under these new rules. Walter had no choice. He had to buy Scottish.

That summer he made his purchases and in came The Goalie, Andy Goram who was soon to establish himself in the Ibrox Hall of Fame, left-back Davie Robertson and midfielder Stuart McCall. Andy, from Hibs, and Stuart, from Everton, were both Scottish international players while Davie had been outstanding for Aberdeen over the previous few seasons. For good measure, Walter also brought in Alexei Mikhailitchenko, the Ukrainian who was one of the most skilful stars I have played alongside.

Yet despite the new signings the season did not start as well as we had all hoped. We were out of Europe in the first round when we lost to Sparta Prague on the away goals rule and then we lost to Hibs in the semi-final of the League Cup and people were starting to point the finger at Andy because of goals lost in these two games. He was really down at that stage because he is the kind of player who is always very self-critical. He felt that he had let the team down and he was miserable but I had looked at him in training and reckoned that he would come through all of these early setbacks, which he did. Until Andy arrived on the scene I had been fairly sure that no one could do better for us than Chris Woods had over his time at the club. I was wrong. Andy became a vital player for us and some of the saves he made during his Ibrox career were out of this world. He proved himself one of the best ever Rangers goalkeepers if not THE best. I know that I have never seen a better goalkeeper and I have most definitely never played with one better than The Goalie. David Robertson was another tremendous acquisition because he could get up and down that left side and he could defend and attack and even pop up with the occasional goal. Stuarty was someone you could not say enough about. He worked tirelessly in the middle of the park and, like Andy, he soon pushed himself into the affection of the fans as well as his fellow players. After the slumps at the start of the season we recovered and we won the League again – this time by nine points from Hearts who finished ahead of third-placed Celtic by a point. Again we went through the season with a healthy success rating against Celtic and, while we lost the first game to Hearts during the time the new lads were trying to settle in we won twice against them after that and drew the other match at a time in the season when the Championship had been won.

Again, though, my illness had persisted and injuries too had taken their toll and, while I played in the early rounds of the Scottish Cup, I missed the dramatic semi-final win over Celtic at Hampden and the Final itself when the jinx which had haunted us was finally laid. Goals from Mark Hateley and Ally McCoist gave us a 2-1 win over Airdrie. By now Mo Johnston had moved on as had Trevor Steven in the constantly changing home dressing rom at the Stadium. The one piece of consistency which was there was the form the team continued to show in the League and the determination of every single player to maintain the title-winning sequence even though, even after this fourth successive win, that magical figure of nine seemed far, far over the horizon. To be honest, at that stage none of us were even thinking of the Celtic record. All we wanted to do was create a little piece of history for ourselves and the club and to provide the Rangers supporters with the kind of success they had been starved of before the arrival of Graeme Souness. Now Walter had picked up the baton and the success rate had not slowed down any. The only murmurings of dissatisfaction to be heard came form the supporters who felt we should be doing better in Europe by now. The changes in the rules had affected us and we had also been unlucky on occasions but the fans wanted to see us do better and the very next season we delivered for them.

7

CHAPTER SEVEN

... and the Next Five!

There were not too many changes in the squad for the new season, the second in which Walter Smith was in full command, though Dave McPherson returned from Hearts to slot back into the defence. He was another Scottish international player, of course, with Walter taking on board all the implications of the European Union rulings regarding the limits on foreign players. There is no doubt that this season, the year 1992-93, was the best we ever knew as a squad. It may also have been one of the very best enjoyed by any Rangers team in the long and trophy-laden history of the club.

An awful lot has been said about the lack of success the team had in Europe over the years and Walter came in for a great deal of criticism over that situation. It was unfair for a manager who gave Rangers more trophies during his time in charge than any other previous manager had done. His achievements were fantastic and they came in a period when competition was greater than it had been before and when the transfer market had moved into overdrive, when the Bosman ruling changed everything, and when the job of running a club had grown enormously.

In any case, that year, the one I am writing about now, proved Walter's credentials in Europe beyond any doubt. There were other seasons when things did not go our way, often because of the run of injuries which the demands of the domestic game always spawned and sometimes, too, because, as was the case against Juventus and Ajax, we met superior opposition. During the inaugural year of the Champions League, however, we had an extraordinary run in the tournament when we went 10 games without losing and when we were within touching distance of a

76

place in the European Cup Final against AC Milan. The French champions, Marseille, just beat us to that place and later they were stripped off the trophy when bribery allegations were proved against the club and its flamboyant owner, Bernard Tapie.

Part of these changes were connected with their game against CSKA Moscow in our Champions League group but it was no help to us.

By the time the investigations were completed and action was taken by the football authorities nothing could be done about the tournament except, of course, the stripping of the title from the French side long after the competition had been over. It was galling for us to realise that, to some extent, we appeared to have been cheated out of our right to play in the Final. We had earned that right, too. We won both our preliminary games before we were placed in the first ever Champions League situation. At that stage the league set-up replaced the quarter-finals and semi-finals. The eight remaining clubs were put into groups of four, thus guaranteeing three more home games. It was not as big then as it has become now but these were the first fledgling steps taken by UEFA to placate the major European clubs who wanted change and who wanted that to encompass more guaranteed fixtures and, therefore, much more revenue from home games.

We were drawn against Lyngby, of Denmark, in the first round and, while it was once looked on as a fairly easy ride when you were drawn against a Danish side, their victory in the European Championship Finals a few months earlier had proved they were an emerging power in world football. Still, we were able to win at home where Mark Hateley and Pieter Huistra scored our goals and then, in Copenhagen, Ian Durrant scored the one goal in our away leg and we were into the second round – something which suddenly became more complicated than it should have been. Initially we were drawn to play the German champions, VFB Stuttgart, who had beaten Leeds United. Then the Elland Road club put in a protest because Stuttgart had named an extra foreign player in their squad for the game. A replay was ordered in Barcelona, Leeds won that and the stage was set for the game which was billed by the tabloids as the Battle of Britain. Naturally we were written off whenever it became clear that we would take on Leeds. But what the writers and telly commentators down south did not realise was that when the play-off had been announced we were all sitting back at Ibrox rooting for Leeds. They were the opposition we wanted. We recognised, before all the jibes started, that if we could defeat the Premiership champions then the people down south would have to take us seriously. It had happened before, also in a Battle of Britain European Cup game involving Leeds.

Then the opposition had come from Celtic and they defeated Don Revie's team in the semi-finals of the competition. Now it was our turn to demonstrate that Scottish football was not the tiny backwater so many Englishmen believed it to be. It was not only the Scots at Ibrox who had a point to prove. Mark Hateley and Trevor Steven wanted to show that they were still operating at a high level despite what outsiders might think of the Scottish League. Trevor had remained in the English international set-up but when Mark returned from Monaco to Rangers his claims were ignored. That was wrong. Big Mark was a marvellous player for the club and against Leeds he had the chance to show England what they were missing. He took it. And he took it in both games!

The two matches were among the best I have ever taken part in during my career. There was an incredible build-up before they came along and when we took the field for the first game, which was at Ibrox, the sound was unlike anything I had experienced before. Old Firm matches always produce a wall of sound, but this was even more intense than anything I had experienced in the games against Celtic. The players spoke about it afterwards and we all agreed that we had not heard anything remotely like that before. It was obvious that the fans were up for the game every bit as much as were were. There were more than 43,000 supporters at Ibrox that night and they sounded like six times that number. That should have had the effect of stopping Leeds in their tracks but somehow or other they came through that sound barrier and struck with an opening goal before a minute had been played. It was Gary McAllister who scored with a long-range shot which gave even Andy Goram no chance of making a save. And in that instant everything went silent. The change in the Stadium was unbelievable and for us on the field, unforgettable too. There was just this deathly hush and then I remember hearing this one wee voice shouting "Come on Rangers, come on" and the crowd picked it up and that deafening noise began again as the support willed us back into the game. We came back too. All the dressing room camaraderie, all the team spirit which had been fostered over the years, all the determination to win against the English champions and to prove ourselves against them combined to haul us back from the dead and give us victory.

Their goalkeeper, John Lukic, punched a corner from Ian Durrant into his own net, Ally McCoist helped himself to a goal and there we were, after summoning up all our ability, all our skills, all our passion, we had won the game. What we hadn't done was win over the English commentators who continued to short change us. I remember Gary Lineker on television after that game when he was asked to look forward to the return match at Elland Road and from the way he spoke it was clear that he had decided it was only going to be a formality. There were newspaper cuttings coming up from down south, too. Our assistant manager, Archie Knox, was getting them sent up and he was putting them on the board in the dressing room where we could read them. They all said the same thing, more or less. We were cannon fodder for the Leeds team, there was really no point in making the journey south simply to embarrass ourselves and on and on they went, bad-mouthing us and refusing to give us any credit whatsoever. Okay, we knew that Leeds were a very powerful team, knew that their manager, Howard Wilkinson, had been able to beat Manchester United to the Premiership title the previous season and knew that they had a group of superb players. There were the Scottish international stars, Gordon Strachan and Gary McAllister, the English pair of David Batty and Tony Dorigo, the Welshman, Gary Speed, and the mercurial Frenchman, Eric Cantona. Still, we had faith in our own ability to withstand any challenge they put up and there was a feeling that when Leeds pushed forward there would be several opportunities available for us to hit them on the break in the classic European away-from-home style and we also believed that in Mark Hateley and Ally McCoist we had the strikeforce who could exploit these situations when they arose during the game. What we did not expect was just how well

Walter had read that situation before the game when he went through his team talk. Of course, we had The Goalie to thank in the opening minute when he made a magnificent save from Cantona but inside another couple of minutes big Mark had scored and we were on our way to one of the club's epic victories. When Mark broke clear in the second half and crossed for Coisty to get a second we were on easy street, slipping comfortably into the counter-attacking style we had operated in the previous away tie against Lyngby in Denmark.

I can remember coming off the field and the Leeds supporters applauding us even though their own team had lost an undefeated home record which had stretched for more than 30 games. These supporters gave us the accolades we had not received from the English Press and television. That meant a lot to all of us. What meant even more, naturally, was that we were now moving into the first Champions League and when the draw was made we avoided AC Milan – which we had hoped to do – but found ourselves in with Marseille who had defeated us in a pre-season friendly at Ibrox. They had some really good players back then, Didier Deschamps was there and Fabien Barthez and Marcel Desailly and Basile Boli – a better player with them than he ever was with Rangers, by the way – and Rudi Voller was their main striker with Allen Boksic as his partner up front.

When they went two goals up against us in the first of the group matches at Ibrox I wondered if we could come back. I was injured and sitting out the game along with Coisty and after Boksic scored in the first half and Voller added a second not too long after half-time Goughie limped off injured and we were up against it. I still don't know how the lads did it, but they hung in and in the closing 12 minutes substitute Gary McSwegan and big Mark both snatched goals and for the remaining time it was the French team who were hanging on the ropes. It was an incredible comeback and a vitally important one. If we had lost the first game at home then we could have forgotten all about the likelihood of qualification for the Final itself. The Group would have been over as far as Rangers were concerned after just 90 minutes. When the second game came along, therefore, we knew that the door remained open and with the Russians of CSKA Moscow having to play their games away from home because of the winter shutdown in their own country, we knew that we did not have to travel there with all the complications that length of journey involves. The venue selected by UEFA and the Russians was Bochum in Germany and that suited us and our travelling support who turned up in their thousands to brave a bitterly cold winter's night. I had shaken off the knock which kept me out of the Marseille game and I scored the one goal which allowed us victory. Mark Hateley held off a challenge from one of the Russian defenders. The big man touched the ball back to me and I struck it well and it took a little bit of a deflection and spun over their goalkeeper and dropped into the net. That goal arrived in quarter of an hour and it was enough to give us an important win away from home.

My injury problems persisted and when the next game loomed in the spring, an away tie against FC Bruges, I was getting treatment. Richard Gough and Trevor Steven were also out and yet the lads returned home with a 1-1 draw thanks to a goal from Pieter Huistra. We had been trailing to a goal they grabbed in the first half and Pieter's strike was close to the end and yet we had had other marvellous chances particularly from Dave McPherson and Stuart McCall which their keeper had somehow been able to reach. The draw, however, was a creditable result with the Belgians now set to travel to Ibrox for the return in two weeks' time and as CSKA had drawn in their "home" game in Berlin against Marseille we still shared the leadership of the section with the French champs. None of this helped my own particular case, though. My injury persisted and when Bruges came to Ibrox I was still marked absent, though Goughie was back even though he was still nursing his injury. Big Mark was unlucky to be red-carded in that game and that kept him out of the crucial match against Marseille in the Stade Velodrome – but it didn't dent our challenge on the night. Goals from Durranty and a spectacular long-range strike by Scott Nisbet gave us the point we wanted.

Now it was a showdown in the South of France and I was fit for this one and for the closing game, too. While we went behind early in the first half Durranty scored not long after half-time and we drew. That left us with the same points as the French team who had to travel to Bruges while we had CSKA coming to Glasgow. We had the easier game but, again, we had to do without big Mark who had been handed a two-match suspension – rough justice in my opinion as the man who had been man-marking him and who had started the incident which led to the sending-off escaped any kind of punishment. That last night CSKA simply retreated deep into their penalty box to defend and on a night when Mark could have made all the difference they survived with these tactics and we were left looking at what might have been. But we gave our supporters a campaign they still savour and will never forget.

It remains there in the annals of the club as one of the most successful forays ever into European competition by any Rangers squad. It was probably the club's best ever chance of winning the European Cup because the way we performed that year, the way we responded to all the challenges which were placed in front of us, we might just have been able to defeat AC Milan as Marseille did with the solitary goal of the game in Munich's Olympic Stadium.

By then, of course, we were preparing for the Scottish Cup Final and the last trophy of the domestic treble. The League Cup had been won early in the season when we defeated Aberdeen in the Final at Hampden with a goal from Stuart McCall and an own goal from their central defender, Gary Smith. The Pittodrie team chased us hard all that season. They finished second in the League and were our opponents in the Scottish Cup Final which was now to be staged at Celtic Park because of renovations being carried out at Hampden. The League was won a month or so before the end of the season when we beat Airdrie at Broomfield with a goal by Gary McSwegan which swept us into the record books. That was our fifth title win and it equalled the previous best club run which had been set up between 1926 and 1931. When we beat Aberdeen in the Final it meant that we had won all the domestic honours and Neil Murray and Mark Hateley scored the goals we needed to round off a season which had been so gloriously successful, even if it did carry its disappointment, too, over the manner in which the Champions League challenge ended. Still, if we thought that was something to feel sorry about, we found Europe to be an ever sadder place early the following season when we were out of the Champions Cup before the league sections were formed. It was a disaster for us against the Bulgarian champions, Levski Sofia, who had surprised us at Ibrox when we had beaten them narrowly by 3-2 with our goals being scored by Dave McPherson and Mark Hateley who helped himself to two. Over there we were drawing 1-1 thanks to a goal from our European specialist, Ian Durrant, until the game was edging into injury time and then one of their players picked up a ball something like 45 yards from our goal. He looked up and you could sense he was ready to have a go and didn't have a hope.

A goal seemed so unlikely that I can remember saying to myself as he lined up "Go on, shoot, shoot" and then he did and he could never have struck a ball better in his life. It sailed into the top corner past Andy Goram and, honestly, there is not a goalkeeper alive who could have reached that ball. It was a pure fluke. The guy could try that again a hundred times and never strike it as well. That night, however, it worked for him and we were out of Europe before we could begin to capitalise on all we had learned the season before. It was a nasty blow.

As Alex Ferguson used to tell his players at Aberdeen when they went out of a tournament early – all we had to look forward to on a Wednesday night now was *Coronation Street*! And that was no kind of consolation after the heady atmosphere which had surrounded Ibrox when we had played Leeds, Marseille, FC Bruges and CSKA Moscow.

Yet between the two games in Europe we found a little bit of form at home which helped sustain us. We beat Celtic in the semi-final of the League Cup – Mark Hateley scored – and the following month went on to win the trophy against Hibs in the Final. This time the goals in a 2-1 win came from Durrant and McCoist with Coisty scoring just a few games after returning to first-team duty after suffering a leg break while playing for Scotland against Portugal in Lisbon. Only he could have done that! It was Aberdeen who put up the main challenge in the League once more and while we beat them at Ibrox, they turned us over at Pittodrie and the two other games were drawn. That helped explain the closeness of the title win that year, with the Dons just three points behind us. That, though, did have a little bit to do with the fact that we lost two of our last three games because we knew the Championship was over. Indeed, we clinched the Championship at Easter Road that season even though we lost the game to Hibs. But we did have a Cup Final to prepare for and the possibility of a back-to-back treble if we could beat Dundee United. That was a game too far for us that season. It was our 121st competitive game over two seasons and the Tannadice team, who had also suffered from a Hampden jinx in their previous Cup Final appearances there, had to beat that one day. The time they chose was against us. Craig Brewster was the man who won the Cup for them on the day. It was the only goal of the match, one that I cannot remember much about, probably because I have tried to erase it from my memory and we were left consoling ourselves with the fact that we had now entered the record books on our own. We didn't have to share billing with that Rangers team of 60 or more years ago who had completed a five title-winning sequence because we had hit six and that assured us of pride of place in Ibrox history. Another treble would have been nice, of course, and another run in Europe would have been even better but the title has always been seen as the major prize at Ibrox and that was very, very important to all of us.

Incidentally, Alexei Mikhailitchenko made a great contribution to the cause that season. He scored two goals against Celtic at Parkhead in the New Year game which gave us a 4-2 win in one of the most thrilling Old Firm matches I have ever watched. Then he scored again to give us a 1-1 draw at Ibrox late in the season. It was a good year for him.

The next season saw the arrival of Brian Laudrup from Fiorentina and the signing of an old European opponent, Basile Boli, who was bought from Marseille. It also saw the team have the most disastrous start to a season that I can remember in all my dozen years at Ibrox. Before the end of August we were a club in crisis. OUT of Europe at the first time of asking again when we lost over two legs to AEK Athens after losing 2-0 in the Greek capital and 1-0 on our own ground. OUT of the League Cup when we were beaten 2-1 by Falkirk, again at Ibrox. And we lost our first League game against Celtic which was also at the Stadium. These were all seriously bad results and when my injury jinx struck again I wondered if things could get any worse. Well, we lost another couple of games to Hibs and to Motherwell before

October was out and we only started putting together some decent form when we beat Aberdeen 1-0 at the end of November. That sent the lads off on a run of nine games without losing which improved our chances considerably. I remember I was back in the team for the New Year game against Celtic and I scored. That gave us a 1-1 draw although the team still had some serious problems which had to be solved somehow or other.

Basile Boli, for example, found it very difficult to adjust to the pace of the Scottish game and to the aggressive nature of our players. The Continental lads don't expect to find themselves being tackled and strongly tackled at that, by front players. But it happens in our game all the time. He didn't like it and he couldn't handle it particularly well. Meanwhile, Brian Laudrup took a little time to play himself in. The European game had come too early for him but we had seen in training what he could do and not one of the players had any doubts that he would be a tremendous success. It's hard to believe now after all the plaudits he received – and rightly so – that in these early months a fair number of the fans were not convinced that he was going to be the answer for us. However, they changed their minds during that season and then were totally converted by the magic he demonstrated in his remaining years with the club. Even in that opening season he scored 10 goals which was only three behind Mark Hateley while Coisty managed just a handful of appearances when he was injured for a long spell. Goughie was out for a while, too, and I think that the efforts of the two previous seasons caught up with several of us. The pressures on players are immense nowadays. There are too many games in a season and you see players suffering from stress injuries more and more. They come from being asked to play too often and when you are successful, the work load becomes even greater and in trying to cope players are much more susceptible to ligament damage, which is one example of the type of injury which has become all to commonplace in the modern game. Recently the Manchester United manager, Sir Alex Ferguson, has been raising this issue and stating that players need to have more of a break from the game – something the current fixture lists don't allow. I don't know if the game will find an answer because teams going into the Champions League nowadays are being asked to play far more games then we did when we were close to making the Final of that tournament. And so it goes on with European Championships and World Cups adding to the number of matches that the very best of footballers are asked to take part in every season. The men who run the game at all levels will have to call a halt some time. I have suffered injuries, so I know what I am saying here.

Anyhow, those are my feelings about what happened to us in the season we went for our seventh successive title. We made it okay, winning by an incredible margin of 15 points from Motherwell with Hibs a point behind them and Celtic, the team I always fear most in every single season, not even in sight. I don't know, though, how we would have coped in that season if we had been battling it out on all fronts as we had done the two previous years. Maybe it was a bonus in disguise when we went out of Europe and out of the League Cup and even out of the Scottish Cup, too, after only a couple of games because our programme was cut back considerably and we were able to concentrate totally on the League games and the reward we could find there and we knew, too, that the ninth title was creeping ever closer as one season melted into another and we were able to maintain our winning streak in the Premier League. It was, however, a season I was glad to see over and done with and I think most of the lads felt much the same.

The next season was to be notable because in the summer the Gaffer went into the transfer market again. Big time! His target was the England international, Paul Gascoigne, who was still playing for Lazio in Italy's Serie A and, just as Graeme had been successful in talking Mark Hateley into giving up the glamour of Monaco, so Walter lured Gazza from the Eternal City and from under the eyes of Premiership clubs who were attempting to buy him, too. It was another master stroke and it was not too long before Gazza was accepted by the support and placed on the same pedestal as Brian Laudrup. Having these two players of genius – and I am not using the word lightly – in the same team meant that the approach we had used over the years had to be adjusted to take into account the individual talents which Paul and Brian brought with them. They were not easily absorbed into any set team pattern. There had to be a certain amount of freedom allowed for both players. They could not be forced into any kind of tactical straitjacket. To do that would have lost you the flair that each of them brought to the team. The fact that Walter gave Brian, in particular, the freedom to do his own thing without being tied down to defensive chores was what brought him the best years of his career. His talents were smothered in Italy, while in Scotland Walter gave them scope to flourish.

8

CHAPTER EIGHT

The End Of An Era …

There had always been changes during the nine years Rangers spent carving out their record-equalling number of title wins. Never a season went past without additions to the squad, which, of course, led to the inevitable departures. For a time when Graeme Souness was in charge it appeared that the dressing room had been fitted with revolving doors, so rapid was the turnover and, also, at times so unexpected.

But as the years wore on Walter Smith was faced with the limit on foreign players which he had to tackle in a rebuilding programme which drafted in Scottish players to enable the strongest team we had to play in European competition. And then, following the Bosman ruling and the relaxation of the restrictions on players moving within the Common Market there had to be a further rethink. After that ninth win – a highlight of our careers – we sunk to the worst season I have experienced as a Rangers player.

There were many reasons for that – team changes which were partially forced upon Walter, decisions which were made regarding transfers and where, possibly, there was little room for manoeuvre for the manager, and Walter's own decision to stand down at the end of the season which he announced to the annual meeting of the club's shareholders in the autumn.

Also we had lost key players in Richard Gough who decided that he wanted to move to the United States to finish off his career there, though he returned to help us out of an injury crisis when the season was just three months old. David Robertson had left under freedom of contract and moved to Leeds United while Ally McCoist and Trevor Steven were both long-term injury victims that year. So was Lorenzo Amoruso who had arrived from Fiorentina and been injured in a pre-season match at Everton and the Swedish international, Jonas Thern, was also seriously injured and made only a handful of appearances. None of these factors helped the team in any way in a season which was so important for all of us.

It is difficult for me to say what went wrong that year, the only season I have been with the club when not a single trophy was won. Some people claimed that when Walter made public his decision to walk away from the manager's job so early in the season it had an adverse affect on the players. I don't go along with that for a moment. In fact, you could look at that announcement in another way altogether and say that the reaction of the squad would have been to make certain that Walter left the club on a high with more trophies to celebrate. I just don't recall any of the lads feeling let down by the news. We were surprised. It had not been something that any of us had expected. Not a single player had an inkling of what was happening until the word filtered back from the annual meeting about what had taken place there. But while there was that feeling of shock I suppose that all of us knew Walter would not go on forever and if he wanted to make his attempt to win the 10th title his last for Rangers then we had to get behind him regarding that objective. I don't believe it became a factor in our failure, though I do believe that perhaps too many changes were made that season and when that was added to the genuine battle fatigue which was affecting many of the players then it all became a title too far for us to win. The galling thing is that we could have won it and, towards the end of the season, we should have won it. It was almost as if Celtic were trying to hand it to us because nerves struck them very badly on the run-in and they stumbled over the finishing line on that last day of the season with only two points of a safety net. It was enough, of course, to end our sequence and yet there were some things which might have allowed us to go on and create a totally new record for Scottish football as well as for Rangers.

I thought it was wrong to allow Paul Gascoigne to leave for Middlesbrough at a crucial period of the season. I can understand why that happened. The season before the Chairman had been very courageous in turning down a huge bid for Brian Laudrup from Ajax, of Amsterdam. The Dutch club wanted him and they knew that the following summer his contract was up and that he could leave Rangers without a fee being paid. That was why they tried to tempt the Chairman who stood firm and decided that Brian would stay. Now he was caught in a similar post-Bosman situation with Gazza and, in business terms, he could not turn his back on another major cash offer and risk losing the player to another club for nothing.

As a player, though, I felt that Gazza – even though he was not playing at the peak he had reached in his first two seasons with the club – was still someone who was capable of winning a match for us with just a few minutes of his individual brilliance. There were games when he did it that year but they were, admittedly, fewer than they had been before. But my thinking was always influenced by the knowledge that he COULD turn it on and he could turn it on better than any other single player in Scottish football. There was no argument about that. Though, I suppose, nor was there any business argument which could be raised against the threat of losing Gazza to another club without receiving a penny piece for him after the club had made a massive investment in the transfer fee to Lazio and his salary over the two and a half seasons he was at Ibrox. Also, there was the evidence too that playing out a last year brought its own difficulties as Brian Laudrup displayed. He was not his usual self either, probably because of the uncertainty about his own future and when he decided halfway through the season to sign a pre-contract agreement with Chelsea then there were obvious signs that the campaign was not going as well as we might have hoped …

These two major distractions did much more to damage the cause than Walter's decision to leave the manager's office at Ibrox.

Over the previous two seasons these players had been the men who had delivered for us in important games. Okay, I know that there were times when they did not do as well as some people expected, particularly in the Champions League when Gazza twice found himself red-carded, once against Borussia Dortmund and once against Ajax which left us weakened in these matches and then in the follow-up games when he was suspended. And the man-marking which Brian was subjected to in the games in Europe was difficult for him to beat. That is a part of the game where the Europeans excel. They have players with a certain discipline who will happily go out and just sit on an opponent, never moving from his side and preventing him finding space. The best players in the world find it hard to beat that and Brian was no exception. He had been subjected to these negative tactics in Italy when he played in Serie A and he had not enjoyed his football there. Coming face to face with them again was not something he enjoyed.

I would never criticise either of the two star players because they did bring us success and they did help us win trophies. It was only in that very last season that the glory run came to an end and I suppose if I am going to be honest I would have to say that all of us knew that there would be a season when it would stop and when the Championship trophy would be removed from the Ibrox Trophy Room for the first time in a decade. Not that this knowledge made it any easier to accept when that day arrived on May 9, 1998. It was a strange season altogether and even when I reflect upon it is hard to come to terms with what happened.

As an indication of the crazy form we were showing you can look at back-to-back domestic results against Dundee United in the early part of the campaign. In the League we defeated them 5-1 at Ibrox with Marco Negri scoring all five goals. A couple of weeks later we played them in the League Cup, also at our own ground and we lost by the only goal of the game. Certainly injuries had forced us to make one or two changes in the team but nothing which should have brought about such a drastic turnaround in fortunes for the club. That was the first of the domestic trophies to go and while we were able to come out on top against Celtic – who had a new coaching staff in the Dutchman Wim Jansen and their former midfield player, Murdo MacLeod – in the first two of the Old Firm meetings with a win and a draw we recognised that they were to be a major danger again. They defeated us at New Year but it was against other teams that we were discovering problems. The form was perplexing, For instance, we beat Dunfermline 7-0 the first time we met them in mid-October and after that in three more games we drew twice and were only able to win the last one at East End Park with great difficulty by 3-2 at a time when we were attempting to put Celtic under pressure at the top of the League. We went on a run of four games without a win at the end of February heading into March, drawing with Kilmarnock, Hearts and Dundee and losing to Motherwell. Those were not the kind of displays we needed though we were able to lift ourselves to gain back-to-back wins over Celtic in the Scottish Cup semi-final and in the League. That gave us a psychological advantage as well as opening up a chance for ourselves to overtake them at the top.

In previous years we would have gone through the end-of-season fixtures claiming win after win because we had become so used to winning titles that it was second nature to us. And, in any case, we knew what was required in terms of commitment because we had been over the course so often before and I was quite sure that the pressure had now moved on to Celtic. They were the team who had to keep their nerve, I felt. They were the team more liable to crack because they had always done so over the nine previous years when the title race had gone to the wire. I have never been so wrong and it still hurts when I remember the team losing 1-0 at Pittodrie the week following the second victory over Celtic. Then, in the second-last game against Kilmarnock at Ibrox we blew it by losing that match by the same single-goal margin.

It should have been finished the next day when Celtic travelled to Dunfermline knowing three points would give them the title. They drew and it went to the last game but while we recovered enough to beat Dundee United at Tannadice they won their game at home and the title-winning era was over for us. All that was left to salvage the season was the Scottish Cup Final against Hearts the following week and while we had defeated the Tynecastle team in three of the League games and had scored 13 goals in the four times we had met and lost just five, and while we were very clear favourites to take the trophy ,we managed to lose that as well by 2-1 at Parkhead.

It was a horrible end to the season and with so many people saying their farewells that night a whole crowd of us just sat there bubbling. Not about the loss of the Scottish Cup that afternoon but about losing the title and about knowing that as in all good

92

things it had come to an end. We were all upset that we had not given Walter a better farewell, of course. After all these trophy victories it was terrible that he won nothing in his last season.

As for myself I can remember sitting thinking about all the players who had made their contributions to the cause, who had helped to put together the most successful period in the history of Rangers Football Club. Davie Cooper had been there for my first season and a bit and he was one of those players who had great skills. He was a naturally gifted winger and he was following in an Ibrox tradition which had always boasted wing men. And which still does today after Dick Advocaat bought Andrei Kanchelskis at the start of the season and then recruited Neil McCann to join him in the team. Coop was one of the special players and we had a lot of these men during the years we were winning.

I've mentioned The Goalie already. He turned himself into a legend at the club and you have to remember that he was taking over from Chris Woods who was the England No.1 and who had been one of the players Graeme Souness built his new Rangers on. Yet Andy Goram went on to surpass Chris and I had not been convinced that anyone had the ability to do that. Andy had great reflexes and tremendous bottle. He is the best I have ever seen at standing up to a forward one-against-one as the opponent comes through on goal. Most times Andy would save or make the forward miss simply by the way he cut down the angles for him. He has got to be the finest technical goalkeeper I have ever seen.

Then there was Terry Butcher, another rock of the revolution set in motion by Graeme Souness all those years earlier. Only Graeme would ever have believed that he could persuade the English international captain to come into Scottish football and, at the same time, turn his back on a possible career with Manchester United. He did it, though, and the big man became a fixture for four years until he decided it was time to move on and he had a spell down south before injury forced him out of the game. But he returned to Scotland to live and he was another player who endeared himself to the support. He had tremendous presence at the heart of the defence and I believe he genuinely loved the atmosphere which surrounded the games. Remember he had spent his club years with Ipswich and the passion he found at Ibrox was a far cry from the normal goings-on at Portman Road. When Terry left John Brown slotted into the centre of defence after playing at left-back and in midfield during his early time with Rangers. Bomber was like myself, of course. He was a Rangers man and while he had played at Hamilton and then Dundee he had always wanted the chance to play at Ibrox. Graeme gave him that and, despite the worries about a long-term knee injury – which apparently had caused him problems on a proposed transfer to Hearts – he went on to play season after season for the club, mostly alongside Richard Gough in an ideal and uncompromising pairing.

It remains a mystery to me and to every other Rangers player who was lucky enough to be one of his team-mates that Bomber was never capped for Scotland. Even towards the end of his career when he was drafted back into the side during yet another injury crisis he was seen by the then England manager, Terry Venables, in a game at Ibrox. Later Gazza told us that Venables had said to him that he hoped that Bomber would not be picked by the Scotland manager, Craig Brown, for the Euro 96 game against England at Wembley. That's how much he admired him – and this was Bomber playing out time in what was to be his last season.

Goughie was a wonderful captain, as I have mentioned already. Also one of the fittest footballers I have known. He had made up his mind to leave when he did despite his comebacks but he was still too good for the game in the United States and while being there has helped recharge his batteries it didn't surprise me that he was able to impress when he returned to Nottingham Forest and now he is back with Walter at Everton. He looked after himself better than any other player I have come across. He always trained very hard and he had his own little fitness regimes which were able to keep him going at an age when other players would have lost their legs.

We had other English international players, too, in Gary Stevens and Trevor Steven who had been together in one of the best of the post-war Everton teams and who slotted in at Ibrox to continue their success in shirts which were a lighter shade of blue. Both of them were under-rated in their time with us. Gary was a tremendously consistent right-back while Trevor moved up and down that wide right channel without ever seeming to tire. Like myself he suffered injuries which had him sidelined for long spells but his crossing and his passing were of pinpoint accuracy and he could help himself to a goal or two when the mood was on him.

But, it cannot be forgotten that the men who made major contributions were not all big-name stars and were not all big-money buys either. Nigel Spackman came in relatively unheralded and performed mightily in the midfield for us. Mel Sterland was in and then out again but did what he was asked to do and covered our defensive emergency situation with a thorough professionalism even though he probably guessed that he had no long-term future with the club. Terry Hurlock was in much the same mould.

Then, of course, we had McCoist and Durrant who had been there pre-Souness and who stayed on until Walter's departure marked the end of their time at Ibrox. Even off the field these two were vital to the success the squad had. They were the sparkplugs in the dressing room. These were the two who kept everything going and everyone appreciated them. Their sense of humour was very Scottish, very West of Scotland in fact, but it could be appreciated by the English lads in the first wave of imports and it was understood, too, by the players who began to arrive from the Continent. To hear Durranty giving one or two of them English lessons was something else. No one else could have done that.

Then Mark Walters and Pieter Huistra kept the wing positions filled after Coop left and we had Mo, Mark Hateley, Stuart McCall and David Robertson and then there were Scott Nisbet and Alan McLaren who were both forced to give up the game after suffering long-term injuries. It's tragic when that happens to anyone but when it's a team-mate you don't know how to handle it. Nissy will always be remembered for that goal against Bruges, of course, while I know that the fans believe that Alan would have been the club captain by this time and there is little doubt that in Scotland terms he would be entering the Hall of Fame in the SFA headquarters. He had won 24 caps by the time he was forced out of the team prior to the European Championship in England in 1996 and he would have more than doubled that total by now and would have played in England and in France at the last Finals of the World Cup. It was a tragedy for both players.

Oh, and I almost forgot to mention the man who kicked it all off and forever changed the face of football in Scotland, Graeme Souness himself. I have written about him as manager of the club but even though he was easing himself out of the playing side when I joined Rangers, he still had all the swagger and style he had displayed with Liverpool. He was one of the outstanding midfield players of his generation and one of the few British players able to go over to Italy and hold his own there in Serie A as he demonstrated with Sampdoria. He wanted Rangers to play in a certain way, in the Liverpool manner, really, and while it was not always possible to do that he never lost his beliefs.

Sometimes I wonder what would have transpired if he had stayed with Rangers. He would not have won more trophies than Walter and more than likely he would have had to face the frustrations when we moved on to the European stage. He would also have been in conflict with the football authorities and that would not have helped him nor Rangers over the years. Maybe he is the type of man who is always that little bit restless and he has scarcely stopped wandering since he turned his back on Ibrox to return to an Anfield he must have found had changed in the years since he was there as a player. He was in Turkey and back in England at Southampton and then left Benfica spectacularly last season. But I don't doubt that he'll be back somewhere because he is a man who is driven to seek new goals to further fresh ambitions. He has been criticised for the way things have gone for him since he left Rangers but even the most vociferous of those who talk badly of him cannot take away the fact that Graeme Souness not only revolutionised Rangers but also dragged Scottish football into the modern age and prepared it for the move forward into the Millennium. If he had not attracted top players, if he had not broken the wage barriers which kept the stars away, if he had not added vital elements of glamour to the Rangers team and forced other clubs to follow his lead then the Scottish leagues of today might resemble those of Northern Ireland. Graeme Souness filled the grounds again and when you look at Celtic recruiting Kenny Dalglish and John Barnes then you have to draw parallels with the Souness arrival at Rangers 13 years earlier. If the Ibrox directors had not acted then, the scenario for professional football in Scotland would be very bleak today. Not only Rangers benefited from his time in charge, the whole game did and supporters of other clubs who complain about Souness should waken up to the facts and realise that. On a personal note I cannot say too much in his praise. He helped me develop as a player by the example he set in games and on the training ground and he gave me the opportunity to play for Rangers. Without him I would not be sitting at home today holding 18 winners' medals won at Rangers (my other Scottish Cup medal, of course, was won with St Mirren before he entered my life) and that is a total which is usually beyond the wildest dreams of any professional footballer.

9

CHAPTER NINE

… and the Dawn of Another

When I signed for Rangers back in 1988 I declared that I would not even look inside the Trophy Room at the Stadium until we had won the treble – that's how confident I felt about success after listening to Graeme Souness outline his plans for the club. It was more than five years before I was able to look at all three domestic trophies on show in the glass cases inside that room which contains so much of the club's history. So much for the feelings of certainty I had when I put pen to paper! Winning the treble is not easy. Under Graeme Souness Rangers were not able to do the hat-trick even once, under Walter Smith we achieved it on that one occasion in 1993 and while desperately close to doing it again the following season we failed at the last hurdle, losing to Dundee United in the Scottish Cup Final.

That tells you a great deal about the squad which was pieced together by Dick Advocaat one summer and celebrated a clean haul of all the domestic trophies less than a year later. It was an incredible thing to do and there were signs as the season reached its climax that this "new" Rangers squad – and it has to be termed that after all the changes which were made at the end of the previous season – may have a great deal to add to the history for the club in the years which lie ahead.

Yet, back in November when we went to Celtic Park for the first Old Firm away game of the season and ended up losing 5-1 I have to say that I could not see the trophy room being full at the end of the season. Until then the team had done well even though they had lost the opening game of the season at Tynecastle to Hearts. Oh, and there had been a little bit of a fright against the Irish side Shelbourne in the UEFA Cup preliminary round. Still, that was a game which came before the season had even begun and when the players scarcely knew each other so that could be understood. The Celtic result came just a few games before the halfway point of the season and it arrived in a game when we had built up a massive lead over Celtic at the top of the new-style Premier League as we pushed for the title.

Certainly we had lost the French international goalkeeper, Lionel Charbonnier, who was injured against Bayer Leverkusen in a European home game, and Lorenzo Amoruso was injured and then young Scott Wilson was ordered off. While we might have coped with a full side it was always going to be difficult to play an hour or so of an Old Firm game at Celtic Park a man down and already goals behind as well. Yet Giovanni van Bronckhorst did score and for spells, even allowing for us being a man short, we pushed the ball around the way the team had been doing for most of the season but Celtic were hungry that day, possibly hungrier than we were because their players knew that if we had beaten them then, even that early in the season, their challenge would have been dead in the water.

I went on as a second-half substitute and I took it badly. Losing to Celtic is not something I have ever been comfortable with, losing to them by that margin was terrible. It was one of the worst days of my life. I hurt today still when I think about it or talk about it. In fact, though it was 4-1 when I went on to the field I still feel a sense of responsibility about the defeat. Of course, it is worse for the Scots lads because they know the rivalry between the two clubs and they know that the supporters will have to take a whole lot of stick at work until the next match gives the team a chance for revenge.

It is, as I say, hard to put a finger on what exactly went wrong because the new players, the lads from the Continent, had been able to handle the tensions that surround the fixture in the game at Ibrox which had ended in a goal-less draw. That day when things went against them and, particularly, when Scott Wilson was red-carded, it was a lot harder than the first game had been. There were a few harsh words spoken in the dressing room afterwards because I was trying to put across the point to the other players of just how much the Old Firm games mattered. Myself and Gordon

Durie were the main spokesmen for the home-based lads and Charlie Miller and Derek McInnes both put in their tuppence worth when training came round on the Monday. I have to say here that there was nothing personal in any of this. We were talking as players always do after a game and, in this case, the result had been bad and so there were certain things which had to be said. Most of the new players understood how we felt.

They knew what we were trying to tell them because most of them had been involved in derby games of their own in various countries though maybe not any quite as intense as the Old Firm confrontations can be. Anyhow, we had a response from Arthur Numan, a smashing player and a tremendous professional, who took it all on board and he said to me that he knew that it had been a bad result and the next time Celtic were opponents the players had to make up for it. But he also pointed out to me that while the result was one that every single one of the Rangers players would want to avenge before the season ended, the really important thing was that we were still at the top of the Premier League, we were still considerably ahead of Celtic and that while they had scored five goals they had still earned just three points from that performance. In essence, he was saying to me that our title challenge had been momentarily affected but had not been derailed to any extent at all. And he was right. Because of the five goals I had lost sight of that when I was doing my thing afterwards and he had a better grasp on the whole picture than I had. At the time I could only think of the result and the goals going in and the way our supporters would be suffering while Arthur was aware of some of that he was also seeing the bigger picture.

When the end of the season arrived he was the man who was right and I didn't mind acknowledging that. It's just that for me the 5-1 result still hurts. It also had me concerned about the remainder of the season even though the squad of players had been doing so well in Europe and had won the League Cup by beating St Johnstone in the Final at Celtic Park. That was the one bad blip on the first half of the season. Sure there were other defeats, the opening day against Hearts I have mentioned and there was another League set-back against Motherwell at Fir Park. In Europe, however, we knocked out the German Bundesliga side

Bayer Leverkusen who were then sitting in second place in their own championship. We were able to win the away tie in Germany 2-1 with goals from Giovanni van Bronckhorst and Jonatan Johansson and then we drew at Ibrox with Jonatan scoring again. That was impressive form and when Rod Wallace scored to give us a draw against Parma at Ibrox we still felt confident about going to Italy for the return.

In the event we went ahead through a superb strike by Jörg Albertz and then had Sergio Porrini red-carded and with only 10 men we lost 3-1 but Parma went on to win the UEFA Cup and that gives an idea of just how the pedigree of the squad was being formed. The result against Celtic had hurt but it had not, as Arthur Numan had indicated, seriously damaged the challenge we had put in for Europe and were still doing in the League.

However, as the season was reaching its climax we began to slip a little and it brought back to mind the horrors of the previous season when we had tossed away points which might have given us the title. By now I was injured after a game against Hearts at Tynecastle which we had won 3-2 to avenge the first-day loss. In successive weeks we lost to Dundee United in the League at Ibrox and to St Johnstone in the same competition at McDiarmid Park and our lead was slowly being eaten into by Celtic. To be honest, I don't think it helped our cause any being forced to play so many live televised games on Sunday nights while Celtic were in action and posting their results some 24 hours earlier than our games kicked off. When they won the pressure was heaped on to us and I did not think that was right. Nor did the Gaffer who had a blast at the number of end-of-season games Rangers were being forced to play at the Sunday night kick-off time which was dictated by television.

Eventually the Scottish Premier League and the television company agreed that the last-day games would all kick off on the Sunday, all of them at the same time to avoid any club having an unfair advantage. That was done – but by the time the games came along they didn't matter because Rangers had already taken the title and had done so in style, clinching our first ever Premier League Championship with a victory at Celtic Park – something which had not been done by any other team in the club's history. The scoreline read 3-0, not as resonant as 5-1 but it was revenge and it was delivered by some of the same players who had suffered the indignity of the defeat in the first Parkhead clash of the season. Importantly though, the game brought the title back to Ibrox, almost as if it had only been out on loan for a season and the squad of players who had arrived, in the main at the start of the season, had been able to make history for themselves. Now they knew it, knew what it felt like to be successful and especially to be successful against the club's oldest rivals. It was a victory to be savoured by everyone at the club.

While the players did their bit on the field I was at the Rangers end with some of the other present-day players and with Coisty and Durrant who had come to see the game. There was criticism of us being there among the supporters but the way the segregation of the support is worked out at Celtic Park the safest place for anyone who is with Rangers or has a Rangers background is in that part of the stand set aside for Rangers supporters. Otherwise you have to sit among the Celtic fans in the main stand and that is not always comfortable when passions run high. While McCoist and Durrant were there that should not be seen as counting against their loyalty to Kilmarnock, a team they helped into Europe last season with Durranty playing so well that he pushed himself back into the Scotland team before the end of the year.

I don't see anything wrong with that and I didn't see anything wrong with the huddle which the players went into right at the end. We had done it when we beat Celtic a couple of years before and the club found itself in trouble with the authorities but what has yet to be said on behalf of the Rangers players is that almost immediately prior to that League game Celtic had beaten us in the fifth round of the Scottish Cup and had broken with their own habit then by having their huddle after the game as well as before it. That rankled with us and our support though nothing was ever said by the people in charge of the game about it taking place. We knew it was aimed at us as a wind-up and when we did the same it was in retaliation. And when the "new" team followed suit they were accused in the Press of inciting trouble when, in point of fact, most of the trouble had occurred much earlier and had nothing to do with the Rangers players or their fans. And when the huddle did take place there were very few Celtic supporters still in the stadium. They had left while our supporters continued to salute the team which had just won the title. The accusations were unfair and the real trouble in that game was in the first half when referee Hugh Dallas had no alternative but to red card Stephane Mahe for conduct which later brought him a reprimand and a fine from his own club.

Following that, of course, the referee was struck by a coin thrown from the Celtic end and was left kneeling and bleeding on the ground. Later Vidar Riseth and Rod Wallace were shown red cards but by that time the game was over, Neil McCann had scored twice and Jörg Albertz had helped himself to a goal and the victory came much more easily than I would ever have believed. It said a great deal for the players that they were able to respond to that hostile atmosphere and to a Celtic team which was obviously going to be very, very determined not to lose the prized title they had won a year earlier, and especially not to do so in front of their own fans at their own stadium. That was something they must have wanted to avoid at all costs. I know I would have felt that way if the roles had been reversed and they were coming to Ibrox to make sure of a title victory.

Anyhow, the doubts which had nagged at me earlier in the season vanished. The attitude of our players was superb and not only that, they overcame any psychological scars which might have lingered from the first Parkhead game. You know, Celtic must have seen that as a springboard to their own ambitions for the season and then, at the ground where they had seen hopes rekindled, they were all lost again. They must have felt the way we had one year earlier and I know how that was.

What was most incredible for me was that seven of the players had either joined almost as soon as Dick Advocaat had taken charge or at some point during the season. Dutchman Giovanni van Bronckhorst, Scottish international central defender Colin Hendry, and the two strikers, the Englishman Rod Wallace and the Argentinian Gabriel Amato, had signed up at the start. They were followed at different times during the season by German goalkeeper Stefan Klos, the captain of the United States World Cup side Claudio Reyna and Neil McCann, who arrived from

Hearts just before the winter shutdown. Incidentally, Neil has to be applauded for the way he has handled the move. He was subject to criticism when he joined us because of his religious beliefs. Unlike Mo Johnston, who was the ground breaker, Neil didn't get much stick from our fans because the Chairman has long since taken down any religious barrier to playing for Rangers and most of the supporters have become accustomed to that and have accepted it.

Still there were times when Neil was being booed from fans of other teams and he handled all of that magnificently. It was not easy for him to come in as he did and carve out a new career but he did so and by the end of the season he had become used to our fans chanting his name and when the Gaffer used him through the middle as an attacker with Rod Wallace in that League game with Celtic he came up with two goals and was able to show everyone that as well as being a natural winger he can also adapt to another role if the coach decides that is necessary. I'd always rated him when he had been with Hearts but he was a revelation over the few months he played with Rangers after his transfer.

I can remember feeling that I was becoming a better player after my own transfer from St Mirren simply because I was playing with experienced internationals all around me. Lots of things rub off on you and that happens when you are the kind of player who is willing to learn. I always placed myself in that category and I think Neil is the same. I am convinced that we are going to see even more great games from him in the future and along with Barry Ferguson, who had a superb season until he was injured, I can see him setting up a partnership which will be of massive importance to Rangers and to Scotland as well because both of them are assured of places in the squads which will be named by Craig Brown for the upcoming European Championship games and well beyond them. That is how good the two players are.

But, to get back to the original point I was trying to make about the influx of players to form the "new" Rangers. It happened before when the European rules were altered and a number of new lads came in while others went out and at the start of that season we were knocked out of the League Cup in the semi-final and out of Europe in the first round because we had not had time to gel, not had time to get to know each other. Yet this time, with even more changes, the "new" Rangers had been able to go out and win a treble in their first season together and to adjust so successfully to the pressure of the Scottish game that they were also able to win the most important and historic of Old Firm games for many years and so write themselves into the record books when their Ibrox careers were only just beginning. It was an amazing feat which underlined Dick Advocaat's tactical sense and his skills in the transfer market.

It was an even more difficult trick to pull than it had been for Walter because on this occasion players were coming into the team who were unfamiliar with the Scottish game. On that previous occasion Walter was bringing in Scottish players, lads who were familiar with the frantic pace the domestic game is played at and who knew the problems that the two Old Firm clubs are always asked to face. Every game is a Cup Final for Rangers and for Celtic. Every team in the country wants to beat you and that was intensified during the long run we had as champions and it was still the same last season when the team was winning the treble. Yet the players came through all the tests which were set for them and I was mightily impressed. There was the odd stumble here and there but when it mattered every player stood up to be counted and no one was hiding from the responsibilities which go with being a Rangers player. You could not have asked for any more than the team gave over the last few weeks of the season.

They won the League and then as a climax to the whole year they also took the Scottish Cup, a tournament which had not always been kind to Rangers over the years and which had given the old guard such a dreadful send-off in the last game we all played together. The tournament had brought some highs and lows with it. Coming back from Florida where we had spent the first-ever winter break training in warm conditions and playing a couple of games we defeated little Stenhousemuir at Ibrox but whether were was a rustiness caused by the three-week gap in competition or whether it was a game the team, understandably, thought they would win easily, the 2-0 result was not one we were going to boast about. Other clubs in the Premier League who had also enjoyed the shutdown struggled more than we did and were out of the Cup early. The next game saw us play Hamilton and while there were the usual confident noises coming from the Lanarkshire club there was no sign of a hangover and Rangers scored six goals to take another step towards Hampden where the huge re-building programme was to be finished in time to stage the Final. Next time out we struggled again to defeat Falkirk 2-1 and then were asked to face our first Premier League opponents, St Johnstone, in the semi-final.

The week before that Celtic Park meeting we lost 3-1 to Saints at McDiarmid Park. That was the fifth time we had played them and while we had started off at Ibrox with a 4-0 win and went on to score seven goals against them in the next game at their ground things had become tighter following these two games. The next time we played each other was in the League Cup Final when we won 2-1 and the next League game saw us squeeze through by the only goal of the game when Sergio Porrini scored. When they defeated us in the match before the Final they must have had the feeling that they had found the secret of playing against us because in each and every game, they had shown improvement. They were confident, of course, and I suppose after the McDiarmid Park game they had every right to be. In spite of the two very serious defeats they had suffered at our hands they were on course for their best-ever season with the possibility of a second Final appearance looming.

The manager stuck, in the main, with the players who had lost in Perth. It may well have been the old managerial attitude that asks the men who have put you in trouble to get you back out of it. Colin Hendry returned after a spell out through injury and that was the sole alteration made and yet the players won 4-0 with the goals scattered through the team with Giovanni van Bronckhorst, Neil McCann, Rod Wallace and then substitute Jonatan Johansson getting himself on to the scoresheet (incidentally, Saints did enjoy one of their best-ever seasons when they finished in third place in the League and qualified for the UEFA Cup adding that to their League Cup Final appearance and their Scottish Cup semi-final match). As for me I was still fighting to recover from injury and now I found myself looking towards that Scottish Cup Final date of May 29 some seven weeks away and wondering if I would get fit in time to bid for another medal. Before that the title was won and the next week the club secretary, Campbell Ogilvie, was able to tell me that I had qualified for another medal because I had played in 10 of the games and that was added to the League Cup medal which I had won after being involved as a substitute in that match. But with the treble a possibility I was desperate to be involved but I knew that it would be touch and go. And that is how it turned out for me because in the week before the Final I was convinced that I would not be playing and I didn't expect to be in the squad.

When I was part of the squad of players who went to Gleneagles Hotel to prepare for the game against Celtic I could not believe it to begin with. I thought that the Gaffer was just doing that to give me a little bit of a gee, to make me feel a part of things, and maybe, also, to help the others because I was one of the few players who had experienced Scottish Cup Finals at Hampden and I reckoned that if any of the lads wanted to ask what they might expect on the day then I would be able to pass on to them the kind of thing I had known in the past and which would help them relax and adapt to the tension.

Cup Finals bring their own tension but an Old Firm Final had added baggage and following the problems which had erupted at the last League game every eye was focussed on this game. It was seen by the football authorities and the police and the politicians as being potentially explosive. The clubs and the players had been warned about on-field behaviour on the day and the supporters had been warned that there would be a huge police presence at the game. And, of course, this was the opening of the new-look Hampden, the National Stadium which had been completed just in time to house the last Cup Final of the century. In one way the Old Firm meeting in that game was something that the stadium committee must have been delighted with. It meant a sell-out game and it meant incredible television exposure even though the downside was the fear of trouble in the stands and around the stadium. Over the years I had been involved in a whole lot of games which had been pin-pointed as high risk and so it would have been natural to have someone around the squad in the build-up who could talk about such things. I didn't dream for a moment that I was going to be named in the squad of players for the game itself. All I had had in the way of matches were two appearances in the reserve team since being hurt against Hearts the week before Christmas. I had travelled to Florida for the winter training there and had been unable to work full-out with the lads and so there was an operation on my return. After that, weeks of rehabilitation and finally the games, one against Kilmarnock Reserves at Ardeer Recreation's ground where I played for about an hour and then another against Dundee Reserves at Creamery Park, Bathgate, when I was in action for 70 minutes.

These surroundings were light years behind the state-of-the-art stadium into which the old crumbling Hampden had been transformed. All of these things simply reinforced my view that I was only along for the ride to Gleneagles and the Final was out of my reach. Then, the day before the match, my whole life changed dramatically and totally unexpectedly when I was told that I was going to be in the squad for the Final. It all happened when the team went for a walk in the grounds of the hotel about 11 o'clock in the morning. Afterwards, around half past eleven, the Gaffer announced the players who would be in the squad for Hampden and I was one of them. Okay, I had only made the bench but it was way ahead of anything I had expected and I knew that if we could win the match then I would have helped at least a little in winning another treble and my collection of winners' medals would be boosted still more. Also, while I had missed out on the Parkhead victory, if we could lift the Cup then that was going to allow me some little personal revenge for the 5-1 defeat back in November. Suddenly the world seemed a different place. The guys always kid me on about being a bit of a moaner but when I'm injured I'm worse and that season had not been easy for me at all. Yet, now, I seemed to be getting a chance to win a medal and even though I had been out for a spell I knew that I was ready for this one if I got the opportunity to go out on to the field.

As well as the talk of trouble the pre-match spotlight had been focussed on the referee, Hugh Dallas. There had been suggestions that he should be replaced by another official following the scenes at Parkhead in the League match. Mr Dallas had been named to take charge of the Final before the League game had taken place which was normal procedure of the Scottish Football Association who used the Final more or less as a prize for the most consistent referee of the season. There were many reasons why the change should not have been made. It would have looked as if the authorities were giving into the hooligans who had attacked the referee and that could not be seen to happen. Or, worse still, it would suggest that the referee had not handled the first game in a proper manner – something which would have undermined his position and maybe his entire future career. Mr Dallas himself was brave enough to say he would not back out.

Before the Final his status as a referee had been underlined by UEFA when they appointed him to control the UEFA Cup Final in Moscow. When it came to the Hampden game he made few mistakes and when there was one decision late in the game when he had to make a judgment call he did so and he did it correctly. Celtic fans screamed for a penalty when a shot was blocked in the penalty box by Lorenzo Amoruso as we were hanging on to our one-goal lead which had come in the first half when Rod Wallace, the bargain signing of the season, had scored. I had had a clear view of the incident from my position on the edge of the box – I had been brought on as a second half substitute – and the big man had taken his arm well out of the path of the ball and allowed it to strike his body cleanly. Later television pictures confirmed that the referee had been absolutely correct and that there had been no doubts at all surrounding that one moment which might have altered things if the referee had not been so accurate in his assessment.

As for the rest of the game, the Gaffer again surprised the opposition when he pushed Derek McInnes into the midfield to give him his first start of the season. He had been out on loan down south and when that period ended he came back to Ibrox and found himself being named regularly among the substitutes during the last few weeks of the season. But, like myself, he was unprepared for the decision which carried him straight into the team. If Derek was surprised then you can imagine how Celtic must have reacted when the team sheet reached their dressing room half an hour before kick-off. They could not have looked for Andrei Kanchelskis being placed on the bench and yet this was one of the decisions which helped us win the game. Derek stopped any threat coming from Regi Blinker and found time to stop some of Stephane Mahe's dashes forward. He was perfect in his role and was one of our best players on that marvellous afternoon. Then big Lorenzo handled Henrik Larsson magnificently while Jörg Albertz was able to muffle the menace from Lubomir Moravcik in another of the midfield battles. Tactically the Gaffer got it right and when Celtic did find a way through as, inevitably, they had to do on a few occasions they found Stefan Klos having his best game since joining the club.

It had been difficult for Stefan after he joined in December. The punters had had to adjust to the loss of Andy Goram, their hero, but had become to accept Lionel Charbonnier when he was injured in that game against Bayer Leverkusen in the UEFA Cup. The Frenchman had started to win over the support and Stefan had then to come in and replace not just one but TWO goalkeepers in their memories – Charbonnier as the most recent star and Goram as the icon of so many previous years. Stefan was safe throughout and I know it meant a lot to him that he had helped Rangers win two major domestic trophies during the five months he had been at the club. He had played his first game on Boxing Day against St Johnstone in the League at Ibrox and his last at Hampden and between them had managed to squeeze in two winners' medals and a whole raft of experience he will be able to draw on in the seasons which are in front of him. To taste an Old Firm Final and an Old Firm League decider in your first few months in Scotland is something that few other players have ever managed to do.

But, if there was someone I was really delighted for that day then it was Lorenzo Amoruso because he had fought his way back into the hearts of the fans after a dodgy start which saw him being jeered during some games. It became so bad that the big man was talking about asking for a transfer and returning to Italy rather than hear his own club's supporters booing him. He was hurt and that was obvious and I was one of the players who knew how he felt because I had gone through the same things at one spell of my own career with Rangers. Hey, you expect to be booed by the opposing fans and if you are then you think to yourself that you

110

must be doing your job properly and shrug off any of the insults that you hear – and you do hear them even at the noisiest grounds – but you can't walk away from them when you hear them coming from your own people. There is not a lot you can do. The only course available is to get your head down, concentrate on your game and give it your best shot until the fans change their minds. I had to do it and Lorenzo did it as well. There were some fans who thought he should not have been named captain and their were some who started to blame him for every mistake made in the defence. He rose above it all. By the time the season ended he was a hero, a captain who had made Rangers history and who was proud of that fact and proud to be a part of the club and its tradition.

No one deserved the accolades from the support after that Hampden victory more than Lorenzo did. His first season had been miserable as he spent most of his time trying to shake off an injury he had picked up in a testimonial game at Everton before any of the competitive games had started. Then when he did come in for a full season he found himself criticised. He must have been surprised by that but he had the strength of character to assert himself and to become one of a handful of Ibrox captains to lead a team to the hat-trick of League, Scottish Cup and League Cup wins and he will be recalled as the first captain to win a Championship at Parkhead and the skipper who took the team to that Scottish Cup win in the first Final to be played at the new National Stadium. Not a bad little mention in the Rangers history books for Lorenzo, is it? Oh, and by the end of that season all of his critics had been silenced, so he couldn't have asked for anything much better than that now, could he?

In that Final though, everyone was a hero and the team will always be remembered for what it achieved after less than one season together as a unit. It was: Stefan Klos; Sergio Porrini, Colin Hendry, Lorenzo Amoruso (captain), Tony Vidmar; Derek McInnes, Jörg Albertz, Giovanni van Bronckhorst, Neil McCann; Gabriel Amato and Rod Wallace with myself, Andrei Kanchelskis and Scott Wilson on the bench but all on the field at the end of the 90 minutes. Andrei replaced Sergio when he was injured and I went on for Neil McCann when he took a knock and Scott took over from Gabriel for the closing couple of minutes as we tied up the game and made certain that the Cup was returning to Ibrox. The celebrations that night were in stark contrast to the tears which had been shed a year before. Then the past was being put to one side, not to be forgotten, never to be forgotten I suppose, but still it was a time which was over. Finished. And all of us knew that. This year we were celebrating a marvellous season but also toasting a fresh beginning, the dawn of a new era, if you like. Because this team has now been tested in the fiercest of games and come through as winners. I can only see the side becoming better and better as Dick Advocaat continues to improve his squad and the players fully absorb the lessons they learned so quickly.

10

CHAPTER TEN

Tributes

It may be difficult to believe now that Ian Ferguson has become so closely identified with Rangers Football Club that he did, indeed, have an earlier existence. As a young S form player with Aberdeen when his namesake, Alex Ferguson, was in charge at Pittodrie. As a senior with Clyde when his manager there was the present Scotland team boss, Craig Brown. And as Scottish Cup Final hero with St Mirren when Alex Smith was the man in charge.

Not only did Fergie play with two senior clubs before eventually making the move to Ibrox that he wanted so much, he was honoured by Scotland at Under-21 level and won a Scottish Cup medal when his goal at Hampden gave the Paisley club victory over Dundee United in the 1987 Final, which was played less than a year before he signed for Rangers in a transfer deal which eventually gave the Love Street club a total of £934,000 in cash once Ferguson had played a certain number of first-team games and duly won his first senior cap for Scotland against Italy in Perugia in the middle of his first full season as an Ibrox player.

Here are the views of five of his managers, all men who had a powerful influence on the career which has brought him so many medals and carried him into the football history books ...

CRAIG BROWN, the Scotland international team manager who gave Fergie his first senior opportunity with Clyde:

"I cannot speak highly enough of Ian Ferguson as a player. He came recommended to me through someone at Clyde because, if I remember correctly, he was working with Dunn and Moore. But I had also received a telephone call from Alex Ferguson who told me that he had released a young lad who had been playing with Aberdeen Boys' Club in the Glasgow area. He thought that the player had talent but the Boys' Club team was being disbanded and, also, he had thought that the laddie was too slightly built and that he might not be strong enough for the Premier League. Yes, we are talking about the same Ian Ferguson! Most people just don't believe that part of the story when they look at Ian in action now and, really, in all the years he has been at Rangers. But he will tell you himself that back then he was slightly built.

"I think he would have been about 16 years old when he started to fill out and from then on he was not the kind of lad you would mix it with out on the field. He always had great confidence in his own ability and that stood him in good stead when I pushed him in to the Clyde team when he was still around 16. He was always ready to listen to advice from the older players, from the experienced lads we had at Shawfield back then, but he was never over-awed by any of them and he never allowed any opponents to get on top of him. Even as a boy he stood up for himself. But it was not only his attitude which attracted you to him as a player. He had good pace, he read games well, with a vision you expected from older players, and he would get forward for you and have a shot at goal. And, always, from the very start he had this aggression that you need in the modern midfield game.

"If I have regrets about the way his career has gone it is only that I have not been able to select him often enough for Scotland. Injuries have hampered him over the years and it is a tragedy that he has won only nine caps for his country. I can tell you now that if he had been fit enough to play in the European Championship in England in 1996 then he would have been there and I think he would have been just the man to mark his Ibrox team-mate, Paul Gascoigne, in that match we had at Wembley. The same goes for the last World Cup Finals in France because, again, he would have been one of the first players listed in my 22 if he had been 100 per cent fit. He wasn't, unfortunately, and so he missed out on these two major events and Scotland missed out on his very special midfield skills.

"I'll tell you something interesting about Ian Ferguson. He scored for St Mirren in the quarter-final of the Scottish Cup the year they won the trophy and he scored again in the semi-final and then, just for good measure, repeated that in the Final itself. And these goals were all scored with his left foot which people reckon he just uses for standing on. That is the type of thing he could always do just to surprise you. Clyde sold him to St Mirren for something like £60,000 or maybe a little more. But I knew that he was going to become a very important player as he developed and he has proved me correct in that assessment.

"Only the injuries and the illnesses which have plagued him have prevented him winning 40 or 50 caps for Scotland and emerging as one of the greatest players of his generation. He still rates in my book as one of the best professionals I have ever worked with and no one has deserved his club success more than Ian Ferguson because few have worked harder to achieve it."

ALEX SMITH, Fergie's manager at St Mirren:

"Fergie, what a boy he is! You know I can still remember my first real sight of him when I took over as the manager at Love Street. I had gone there when Alex Miller left to join Hibs and on my first day I said to Jimmy Bone, my assistant, to take the players to the training ground they used at that time and to get them started working and that I would come along later and take a look at them during a practice game. I just thought that was maybe the best way for me to ease myself into the job and allow the players the opportunity to start the game without me and so lessen any worries they might have had about a new manager coming in.

"Well, it would not have made the slightest bit of difference to Fergie if SIX new managers had turned up. There he was, out on that field and running the show. At that time you couldn't miss him, of course, because he had these blonde streaks running through his hair. I didn't pick up on who he was to begin with and I turned to Jimmy Bone and asked him who the lad was who was doing all the shouting and he told me that it was the player Alex Miller had signed from Clyde just a month or two before. No wonder I had not recognised him. He was shoving players like Frank McGarvey and Neil Cooper out of his way to get at the ball, and I'm talking about really experienced professionals being pushed to one side as Fergie ran things. I'll never forget that game because it showed me that here was a player with a tremendous appetite for the game, and one who would not walk away from any kind of on-field confrontation. He had a tremendous talent as a boy and that developed as the seasons went by, although while he was a hero in our Cup run and an important player for us in Europe the following season it was Rangers who had his best years and that was largely because of Fergie himself.

"He had his mind made up that if Rangers ever wanted him then he would not be happy playing for anyone else. He gave me a helluva time once the news broke that Graeme Souness was trying to buy him. He was never out of my office, every day I had him in asking me when he was going to be sold and when would he be able to sign for Rangers and, of course, the club were not all that keen on letting him go to another Scottish club. So when it became obvious that he was not going to be happy staying a St Mirren player we let it be known that he was available for transfer and Alex Ferguson, who was at Manchester United by this time, came on the phone to me and said that he wanted to take him to Old Trafford. Then Terry Venables, who had just taken over at Tottenam, made another offer. I told Ian about them and, I think he actually spoke to the other Fergie, but even the lure of Manchester United and Spurs, two of the biggest names in English football, could not tempt him.

"I had always known he was a Rangers man because there would be some kidding around in the dressing room between our players on the subject of the Old Firm – just as it happens at every club in the country. However, it was only when the transfer business came up that I realised just how committed he was. Nothing was going to stop him being a Rangers player whenever he learned that he was a target for them. I knew that I would get nothing but trouble from him until it was all settled and so I told the board that we should try to make a deal which would be as good as we could possibly get in financial terms. I was going to lose a player – but my job as a manager was to get the top price possible. Finally, after months of talking and maybe a hundred knocks on the door from Fergie, the deal was agreed. In the end with all the bits and pieces added – caps for Scotland, appearances in the first team were part of the package – St Mirren received £934,000 which was a tremendous return on their own investment in the player. I believe Clyde finished up with something extra from the transfer money and they benefited in all by £100,000. However, the biggest beneficiaries were Rangers who have now had 11 seasons from a player who became one of the best midfielders we have had in Scotland during the last decade. If he had not suffered illness and injury then there is no knowing what he might have achieved. They held back his international career, for example, and they kept him out of a lot of Rangers games at a time when he was becoming a key player at Ibrox. He had everything you looked for in a midfield player, pace and vision and boundless aggression. I saw that in my first glimpse on the training ground and he has never lost that over the years.

"People will look back on his career and realise just how important a player he was for Rangers in domestic and in European games. Believe me, I am certain that Graeme and then Walter put his name down first on the team sheet when they were about to play a really vital match. Because Fergie was always a big game hunter, he loved the atmosphere and he was never one who would buckle under pressure no matter how severe that might become. And you want to know something else? He was a helluva decent laddie and as straight as you can find anywhere."

GRAEME SOUNESS, the manager of Rangers who bought Fergie and afforded him the opportunity of playing with the team he had supported for as long as he could remember:

"When I first became aware of him he was playing for St Mirren and I liked the look of him from the start. As far as I was concerned Fergie had all the qualities that a modern-day midfield player requires and I knew that we were soon going to need someone to take over my own role in the Rangers team. I realised as soon as I had seen him a few times that he would be able to take on a similar role. What I did not realise was just how forcefully he was going to assert himself when he arrived at the club. In fact, Fergie was the player who convinced me that it was time to hang up my boots and retire from playing and simply concentrate on managing. How that happened was simple – but it gave me a very salutary lesson and one which I acted on as quickly as I possibly could! I was playing in a practice game at the Albion not too long after Fergie had signed for the club. Now one of my own strengths as a player had been my ability to shield the ball and keep people from gaining possession. I had worked on it over the years and I was proud that even when I was reaching the veteran stage I was still capable of holding my own. Or was until Fergie came on the scene. One day as I tried to hold him off he just brushed me aside and went off with the ball. It was something I had done a thousand times before and against some of the toughest players in the world and yet here was the new kid on the block giving me the message.

"That was the moment I knew I had to stop playing. Fergie just spelled it out to me.

"He added some dig to our midfield area but he had more than that to his game. He was quick, he could tackle and he could get you a goal – nothing frightened him. In many ways he reminds me of Roy Keane, of Manchester United, who is one of the most complete midfield players in the world today. He has everything and Fergie did too except that the injuries and the illness problems he suffered while I was still manager at Rangers held him back.

"He suffered because of that and he suffered too, in my opinion – though he will no doubt argue with me on the subject – from caring too much for Rangers. He was a supporter of the club, a dyed-in-the-wool supporter who used to go and stand on the terracing and sometimes he would allow that to interrupt his concentration in a game. He was just so desperate to do well that he would lose his focus on the job he was being asked to do. On the other hand, of course, you knew that he would go into the trenches for you and he did that on any number of occasions in Europe and at home.

"I suppose, looking back, St Mirren held me to ransom because they knew I wanted Fergie so badly and they knew, too, that he just did not want to sign for any other club in the world. Yet when you think of the contribution he has made to Rangers and you realise that for the nine hundred thousand quid spent you had a class player in the team for 11 of the most successful years the club has known in its history, he might just be one of the best signings I ever made while I was in charge at Ibrox. And, after all, I did make a few ..."

WALTER SMITH, who succeeded Graeme Souness as manager and was his right-hand man when Fergie signed and is now boss of Everton:

"Signing Fergie from St Mirren became a little bit of a saga but it was worth going through the agonies to get him to Ibrox as a player. Graeme and I had sat down and discussed the situation we had regarding the middle of the park. We had Ian Durrant in there and Derek Ferguson as well as Graeme himself but we knew that Graeme would not be going on forever and we had to make provision for the time when he would be ready to give up the player-manager's role.

"I am sure that Graeme saw a lot of himself in Fergie, in the aggressive way he approached the game and the strength he had when he was making challenges to win the ball. When he arrived at Ibrox he found out just how powerful Fergie could be as I believe he has told you in this book. Sometimes, though, that aggressive streak has hidden his other talents so that a lot of the fans have not always realised just how good a player and how important a player he has been for Rangers.

"Fergie is a great passer of the ball, he reads the game superbly and he is very, very quick. In fact he is an identikit for the kind of player every club with any kind of ambition needs to have in the middle of the park. It goes without saying that he was utterly committed to Rangers' cause. He still is. Nothing would ever be able to change that as far as Fergie is concerned. There were occasions when some club or other would come on and enquire about his availability when I was the manager. I always take the view that the player involved should be told of any interest in him and I would follow that up by calling the player in and informing him that there was a chance to move if that is what he wanted to do. Fergie's reaction to any such talk was priceless. He would get that really crabbit look on and snarl out a refusal to go anywhere else. You knew that he meant it. He had a way of never leaving you in any doubt on that subject. The highest tribute I can pay is that when I was facing a particularly difficult game then Fergie's name was the first down on the teamsheet because I knew he would never let Rangers down. I think Graeme would tell you the same thing.

"I am just sad that injuries affected him so often. He deserved better than that but he is still, for me, one of the Rangers greats."

DICK ADVOCAAT, the current manager of Rangers and already a treble winner:

"Ian Ferguson is the protype Rangers player. As well as being a model professional he is someone who has been a link between the teams of the past who had so much success and the new team which has started off with winning the treble.

"He has been important because of that, because of his experience, in the dressing room during my first season with the club. It is clear to me and to anyone else who arrives at Ibrox that Ian Ferguson is a footballer who has achieved his ambition by becoming a Rangers player. It is so obvious that he is a supporter as well being a member of the squad.

"I have always found him ready to adapt for the good of the team by taking on certain roles in certain games. He has qualities which very often make him important to the team and which always make him a vital ingredient in the dressing room. It was not out of sentiment that he was in the Cup Final team last season, he was very definitely there on merit. I am very happy that he has stayed with the club during the transition and happy, too, that he was awarded a testimonial game. No one would ever grudge him that honour."

11

CHAPTER ELEVEN

Statistics

Signed: 15/2/88 from St Mirren
Reported fee: £850,000
Debut: 27/2/88 v Dundee United, away, 1-1
(Rangers team: Woods; Nicholl, Bartram; Roberts, Wilkins, Gough; D. Ferguson, I. Ferguson, Nisbet, Durrant and Walters)

TROPHIES WON DURING CAREER

League Championship
1988-89, 1989-90, 1990-91, 1991-92, 1992-93, 1993-94, 1994-95, 1995-96, 1996-97, 1998-99.

Scottish Cup
1993, 1996, 1999
(a Scottish Cup medal was won with St Mirren in 1987).

Scottish League Cup
1988-89, 1990-91, 1992-93, 1993-94, 1998-99.

IAN FERGUSON'S APPEARANCES AND GOALS SEASON BY SEASON

1987-88

League appearances	–	8
League goals	–	1
TOTAL APPEARANCES	–	**8**
TOTAL GOALS	–	**1**

1988-89

League appearances	–	30
League goals	–	7
Scottish Cup appearances	–	6
Scottish Cup goals	–	2
League Cup appearances	–	3
League Cup goals	–	2
European appearances	–	4
European goals	–	1
TOTAL APPEARANCES	–	**43**
TOTAL GOALS	–	**12**

1989-90

League appearances	–	24
League goals	–	0
Scottish Cup appearances	–	1
Scottish Cup goals	–	0
League Cup appearances	–	5
League Cup goals	–	2
European appearances	–	2
European goals	–	0
TOTAL APPEARANCES	–	**32**
TOTAL GOALS	–	**2**

1990-91

League appearances	–	11
League goals	–	1
Scottish Cup appearances	–	1
Scottish Cup goals	–	0
League Cup appearances	–	2
League Cup goals	–	0
European appearances	–	1
European goals	–	0
TOTAL APPEARANCES	**–**	**15**
TOTAL GOALS	**–**	**1**

1991-92

League appearances	–	16
League goals	–	1
Scottish Cup appearances	–	3
Scottish Cup goals	–	0
League Cup appearances	–	2
League Cup goals	–	0
European appearances	–	1
European goals	–	0
TOTAL APPEARANCES	**–**	**22**
TOTAL GOALS	**–**	**1**

1992-93

League appearances	–	30
League goals	–	4
Scottish Cup appearances	–	2
Scottish Cup goals	–	0
League Cup appearances	–	4
League Cup goals	–	0
European appearances	–	7
European goals	–	1
TOTAL APPEARANCES	**–**	**43**
TOTAL GOALS	**–**	**5**

1993-94

League appearances	–	35
League goals	–	5
Scottish Cup appearances	–	5
Scottish Cup goals	–	1
League Cup appearances	–	5
League Cup goals	–	3
European appearances	–	2
European goals	–	0
TOTAL APPEARANCES	–	**47**
TOTAL GOALS	–	**9**

1994-95

League appearances	–	16
League goals	–	1
Scottish Cup appearances	–	0
Scottish Cup goals	–	0
League Cup appearances	–	2
League Cup goals	–	0
European appearances	–	2
European goals	–	0
TOTAL APPEARANCES	–	**20**
TOTAL GOALS	–	**1**

1995-96

League appearances	–	18
League goals	–	2
Scottish Cup appearances	–	3
Scottish Cup goals	–	3
League Cup appearances	–	1
League Cup goals	–	0
European appearances	–	3
European goals	–	1
TOTAL APPEARANCES	–	**25**
TOTAL GOALS	–	**6**

1996-97

League appearances	–	24
League goals	–	1
Scottish Cup appearances	–	3
Scottish Cup goals	–	0
League Cup appearances	–	1
League Cup goals	–	0
European appearances	–	4
European goals	–	0
TOTAL APPEARANCES	**–**	**32**
TOTAL GOALS	**–**	**1**

1997-98

League appearances	–	11
League goals	–	0
Scottish Cup appearances	–	2
Scottish Cup goals	–	0
League Cup appearances	–	2
League Cup goals	–	0
European appearances	–	4
European goals	–	1
TOTAL APPEARANCES	**–**	**19**
TOTAL GOALS	**–**	**1**

1998-99

League appearances	–	13
League goals	–	0
Scottish Cup appearances	–	1
Scottish Cup goals	–	0
League Cup appearances	–	4
League Cup goals	–	1
European appearances	–	9
European goals	–	0
TOTAL APPEARANCES	**–**	**27**
TOTAL GOALS	**–**	**1**

1999-2000
League appearances   –   1*
* as at 1 September 1999

Total For Career

League appearances	– 237
League goals	– 23
Scottish Cup appearances	– 27
Scottish Cup goals	– 6
League Cup appearances	– 31
League Cup goals	– 8
European appearances	– 39
European goals	– 4
TOTAL APPEARANCES	**– 334**
TOTAL GOALS	**– 41**

INTERNATIONAL APPEARANCES

Ian Ferguson has won 9 full caps for Scotland as well as 6 Under 21 honours.

His full international record is:
Italy 2 Scotland 0, 1988
Cyprus 2 Scotland 3, 1989 (as substitute)
Scotland 2 France 0, 1989
Scotland 3 Malta 0, 1993
Scotland 3 Estonia 1, 1993
Malta 0 Scotland 2, 1993
Austria 1 Scotland 2, 1994 (as substitute)
Holland 3 Scotland 1, 1994 (as substitute)
Estonia 0 Scotland 0, match played in Monaco,1997 (as substitute)

THE AUTHOR

KEN GALLACHER is one of Scotland's foremost football writers – and has been for over three decades now.

His respected views on the game are now featured in The Herald and throughout his career the man the players trust has been the top talent at almost every major Scottish title.

When Andy Goram, Richard Gough and Mark Hateley told their life stories they chose to speak to Ken Gallacher. Now "Fergie" is the latest Rangers book from a man who has travelled the world covering both sides of the Old Firm and Scotland.